LOVING
THE WORLD
—— *with* ——
GOD

FOURTH DAY LIVING

REBECCA DWIGHT BRUFF

D0168283

UPPER
ROOM BOOKS®
NASHVILLE

Cover design: Marc Whitaker / MTW Design / http://www.mtwdesign.net
Interior typesetting and design: Kristin Goble / PerfecType

Library of Congress Cataloging-in-Publication Data

Bruff, Rebecca Dwight.
  Loving the world with God : fourth day living / Rebecca Dwight Bruff.
      pages cm
   ISBN 978-0-8358-1335-8 (print)—ISBN 978-0-8358-1336-5 (mobi)—ISBN 978-0-8358-1337-2 (epub)
1. Christian life. I. Title.
  BV4501.3.B777 2014
  248.4—dc23

                          2013049537

For all the Petronas

CONTENTS

ACKNOWLEDGMENTS

God has been beyond generous, and I am beyond grateful.

My deepest thanks go to family, friends, and colleagues who have shared with me this journey of loving the world with God. My sons, Nathan and David Frank, have taught and continue to teach me to stretch and risk and live and love. We've built houses in Mexico together; we've built memories with one another; and I eagerly anticipate whatever the next bend in the journey reveals. They inspire me by just being who they are. My parents, Jerry and Ida Dwight, my sister, Wink, and brother-in-law Gary Mueller have been relentless encouragers. My amazing and brilliant husband, Tom Bruff, inspires and encourages me every day, helps me stay balanced, and keeps me laughing. He is my hero.

One of my life's sweet privileges is to have friends who are colleagues and colleagues who are friends. The wisdom, work, humor, and hearts of Steven Mabry and Marta Nielsen, Donna and Leighton Bearden, Kathy Moseley, Linda and Frank Roby, Rachael and Pat Faubion, Neil Moseley, Kim Brannon, and so many others are spilled on every page.

These adventures in mission began for me with the youth and adult leaders of First United Methodist Church and The United Church, both of Los Alamos, New Mexico, and spread among the congregations of Wesley United Methodist Church in McKinney, Texas; Highland Park United Methodist Church of Dallas; First United Methodist Church of Colorado Springs, Colorado; and University Park United Methodist Church, Dallas, Texas. We were hosted and taught by the good and gracious people of Agua

Prieta, El Pescador, Juarez, and Tecate, Mexico, and at numerous community ministries in Dallas, Texas; Abia State, Nigeria; San Juan la Laguna, Guatemala; Espanola, New Mexico; Costa Rica; Saratov and Novgorad, Russia; and Dulac, Lousiana. The people I met there give evidence to the Incarnate God. I give thanks for the many extraordinary people loving the world with God in all those beautiful places!

These pages provide an inadequate expression of gratitude to God and the people through whom God relentlessly loves the world. Thanks be to God.

FOREWORD

Perhaps you picked up this book because you recognized the term *Fourth Day*, or perhaps you picked it up because you have a passion for loving the world. Either way, I am excited to invite you to share this journey of Fourth Day living. For over fifty years, Christian movements like Cursillo, Tres Dias, and Via De Cristo have been using the term Fourth Day to describe the new and transformed way of living after the shared journey of a three-day retreat. Within all Fourth Day movements, the primary focus is not the weekend retreat itself but the new way of living that comes after the retreat. This is what we call the *Fourth Day*.

The mission statement of The Upper Room Walk to Emmaus and Chrysalis is "Empowering leaders through Emmaus and Chrysalis to be the hands and feet of Christ." Striving to be the hands and feet of Christ in the world is not unique to the Emmaus and Chrysalis movements. Jesus issues this invitation: "As the Father has sent me, so I send you" (John 20:21). Jesus doesn't send his disciples to an isolated retreat; he sends them into the world. Similarly, I find that we can't truly live the mission statement of The Walk to Emmaus and Chrysalis within the bounds of a three-day retreat. Only when the weekend is over can we achieve the mission of loving the world as God does.

For readers who may be unfamiliar with The Walk to Emmaus, Chrysalis, or other Fourth Day movements, they each begin with a seventy-two hour retreat. Attendees come from all over the world and from many different churches. Fifteen talks are shared over the course of the three days—ten given by laypersons on various aspects of living a life of discipleship and five given by clergy persons on the subject of God's grace. Small-group sharing follows each talk. Throughout the retreat, time spent in meditation and worship serves to bring participants to a deeper experience and understanding of their relationships with God as well as their places within the body of Christ. After the weekend, participants are encouraged to continue to meet with their new Fourth Day communities through small covenant groups and larger worship assemblies. The Walk to Emmaus is designed for Christians over the age of eighteen, and Chrysalis is divided into two programs: one for young persons ages fifteen to eighteen and one for young persons ages nineteen to twenty-four.

If you have attended a Walk to Emmaus or Chrysalis weekend, you experienced God's love during your three-day retreat. It is this love that author Rebecca Dwight Bruff encourages you to share as a way of Fourth Day living. After you have experienced God's love, how can you not share that love with your local and global neighbors? Rebecca offers guidance and tangible examples to show how people have embraced the teachings of Emmaus and Chrysalis to transform their lives and the lives of others.

Brothers and sisters from across all Fourth Day movements, join Rebecca on a journey that goes far beyond the confines of a retreat into a world in need of God's love. For it is only in the world that you can move from receiving God's love to sharing God's love.

Kate Dickinson
Associate Director of Emmaus Ministries
Upper Room Ministries

INTRODUCTION

In the spring of 2005, I reluctantly gave in to the urgings of a whole gaggle of friends who insisted that I experience the Walk to Emmaus*. I didn't want to go. Hearing that the retreat would change my life wasn't helpful; I'd recently experienced all the change I could handle and felt like I had pretty much hit my threshold. People told me the Walk to Emmaus would profoundly enrich my experience of God by deepening my relationship with Jesus Christ. But my relationship with Christ was solid. In fact, the unrelenting change of the previous eighteen months had galvanized my trust in God's grace. For a time, it was the one thing on which I could rely. But the well-meaning people wouldn't let it go, so in April, I succumbed, motivated almost exclusively by the desire for them to stop insisting.

It was a good weekend. It didn't change my life, but it made it richer. It didn't galvanize my relationship with Christ—that was already robust— but it enlarged my gratitude. Something surprising happened: The weekend provoked me; it made me ask questions. *What would it be like*, I wondered, *if we all took our call to action seriously? What would it look like if the Christians in our pews on Sundays took their faiths into the world the other 167 hours of the week? How could deeply committed Christians be more intentional, more involved and invested,*

---

*The Walk to Emmaus is an ecumenical spiritual renewal retreat experience designed to strengthen local churches by cultivating Christian disciples, both lay and clergy. It grew out of an adaptation of the Roman Catholic *Cursillo* movement, which originated in 1949 in Spain. *Cursillo*, meaning "little course," provided exactly that—a little course in Christianity. The youth experience of Emmaus is called Chrysalis.

and more useful in making a difference in the world? My Emmaus experience gave me a deep appreciation for the many steadfast disciples of Jesus Christ who are fully committed to the life of the church *in* the church. I began to wonder what would happen if we as Christians were as thoroughly devoted to the well-being of those *beyond* the church. What might happen if we asked and discovered how *to live*, not just what *to believe* or what *to do?*

This book is about loving the world with God—fostering compassionate, courageous lovers; people whose lives are defined and shaped by God. It's about being the church—not the institution but the body of Jesus Christ. This book tasks us with surrendering ourselves to that which we invoke in the eucharistic prayer: "Pour out Your Holy Spirit on us gathered here . . . that we may be for the world the body of Christ, redeemed by his blood."[1] *That we may be for the world the body of Christ*—a community of individuals formed by and around the love of God found in Christ.

Truth be told, I wanted to title this book *So you had a nice weekend with Jesus. Now get over yourself and go love the world already.*

Part I

Living Life on Purpose

"You shall love the Lord your God with all your heart, and with all your soul, and with all your mind." This is the greatest and first commandment. And a second is like it: "You shall love your neighbor as yourself."

Matthew 22:37-39

1

Preparing for Reentry

[The disciples'] eyes were opened, and they recognized him.

Luke 24:31

Last July my husband, Tom, and I joined one of our church's mission teams. We left the blistering, triple-digit Dallas heat on July 28 and spent the next seven days on the shore of Lake Atitlan in Guatemala's cool, green Western Highlands. We reacquainted ourselves with our Guatemalan friends, worked hard, laughed a lot, and experienced spiritual refreshment that mirrored the delightfully cool temperatures.

And then Tom and I returned home to Dallas's sweltering August days. We returned to our daily routines—paying bills and walking the dog and doing laundry. It's not that we weren't glad to be home. But our lives seemed mundane after our wonderful week in a beautiful place doing meaningful things with fabulous people.

Is there anything more invigorating than a mountaintop experience? And is there anything more deflating than the bumpy reentry into normal, everyday life? I wrote this book for those who have been to the mountaintop—an Emmaus weekend or a mission trip or simply a quiet time of sabbath rest—and who now know that God is inviting them to more. Not more work or obligatory busyness but a more authentic connection with God and with God's work in the world. We tasted grace on the mountaintop, and now we thirst for more.

Emmaus and Chrysalis participants report a broad range of experiences and emotions after attending their respective weekends, many of which differed from their expectations. Maybe, like me, they expected a mountaintop experience but instead felt a so-so moment. Maybe, like me, they attended some thoughtful—even thought-provoking—presentations that were mixed with contrived emotional energy and returned home more exhausted than renewed. Maybe, like me, they were delighted that some people had a mountaintop experience, but they endured something more like a difficult hike—good exercise but less than enjoyable. And yet, like me, they caught a glimpse of the gospel's promise.

Maybe we experienced a depth of divine goodness during our Walks to Emmaus or spiritual retreats. Or maybe not. Maybe we received more love—unconditional, mysterious, powerful, tangible love—and we know that we in return want to offer it to others. Or maybe not. Maybe we are now absolutely confident that God is ready to work in us and through us. Or maybe not.

Whatever we experienced and wherever we are in our journeys, is good. Whatever we experienced on the mountain—a peak experience, a test of endurance, a mix of highs and lows—has brought us to this day, this moment, of asking *What's next?*

At the end of an Emmaus or Chrysalis weekend, the retreat staff invite each participant to respond to the following questions: *What has this weekend meant to me? What am I going to do about it?* We could ask ourselves these questions throughout our lives in response to all kinds of events and experiences. We might be wondering what God has awakened in us or what God is nudging us toward. But the world can often be a discouraging place when we seek to follow God.

If we find ourselves on the mountaintop after our weekend retreats, reentry into the real world can be difficult. Perhaps people in our lives haven't lived through mountaintop experiences. They nod their heads as we explain how God has changed and is changing us, but they don't understand. The real world doesn't function like the mountaintop world. People don't sing to us every morning in the real world or surround us with affirmation or provide space for quiet prayer and reflection or engage in long, thoughtful conversations. After we reenter the real world, we begin to long for the mountaintop world where we can focus on our lives with God.

On the other hand, if our experiences were so-so, a mixed bag, or a bit perplexing, we may feel confused and disoriented after reentry. We may struggle with integrating those aspects of our experiences that really meant something to us into our daily lives and letting go of the elements that annoyed us. In either situation—transitioning from the mountaintop experience or identifying the meaningful aspects of a so-so weekend—we face adjusting to the real world after a spiritual journey.

Reentry is difficult, but it also provides an extraordinary opportunity. We've left our designated spiritual spaces, we've come home, and we feel different. Our hearts and minds have encountered God's presence, and now we see everyday activities in a new light. We may not have fully processed it yet, and we may not be able to articulate it, but we know in our bones that something has shifted within us.

Every Day Is Our Fourth Day!

Today is our Fourth Day. Today and every day that follows our mountaintop experiences is our Fourth Day. On the last day of the Emmaus weekend, we heard these words: "These three days have had only one purpose: to prepare you for your Fourth Day, your walk with the Lord every day from now on."[1] Those three days of worship, study, conversation, laughter, prayer, connection, discovery, and reflection center around God's love for us, God's grace for us, and God's Spirit in us.

The last chapter of Luke's Gospel documents the first walk to Emmaus when two disciples encounter the risen Christ. After their encounter, their lives take a new direction. The disciples actually turn around and go a different way because Jesus gave them new perspectives and purpose.

Take a few minutes to read Luke 24:13-35. Imagine the experience of that first Easter afternoon for those two disciples. Reflect on the thoughts, feelings, questions, disappointments, and hopes of those two disciples as they walked the road to Emmaus. Like those first Emmaus pilgrims, our encounters with Jesus give us new perspectives and purpose. We see life differently. God is suddenly present everywhere—even in our questions. Jesus' grace and love are obvious—even in our struggles. We can feel the power of the Holy Spirit rushing through us. And now, like those first Emmaus pilgrims, we have an extraordinary opportunity to share God's goodness and mercy. We possess not only the opportunity but also the mandate to share the good news with others. How will we do this?

Tricia, an Emmaus pilgrim in Dallas, said, " I couldn't *not* do something. I had to find a way to begin to give what I had received!" Tricia reports that in the days following her Emmaus weekend, she began to notice things she simply had not noticed before, and she began to be aware of people in new ways. Like the disciples in Luke's Gospel, her eyes were opened. Soon she was learning about a group that provides meals for homeless women and men in downtown Dallas, and she decided to go along early one Sunday morning.

Tricia's story is not uncommon. People of all ages and experiences often find themselves itching to respond to God's love in tangible ways in order to extend God's goodness and care to others after completing a spiritual retreat such as The Walk to Emmaus. And like Tricia, they find themselves asking, *Where do I start?*

Good news! Our starting place is simple: Our Christian identity—our very being—is grounded in the affirmation that the triune God created the world in love, reveals that love through Jesus Christ in order to redeem and transform it, and through the enlivening presence of the Holy Spirit, empowers Christ's followers to follow, participating in God's mission of loving the world. Jesus himself affirms that his followers are to be a sent people: "As the Father has sent me, so I send you" (John 20:21).

God is ready to send us to love others, and we are ready to be sent. This doesn't mean that we have to go to Afghanistan or Zambia (although we could). It doesn't mean we have to change our vocations (although we might). It does mean that God will send us back into our worlds as ambassadors of Christ's love. It means that our lives—where we live and work—become our mission places. It means that wherever we go and whatever we do, we're reflecting God's care, goodness, hope, and love. We are now responsible for extending and reflecting the love of God.

Does that sound intimidating? Honestly, it should. It should strike us as more than a little challenging because, frankly, it is. It is challenging to be the hands and feet of Christ in the world. It is challenging to love people who are difficult. It is challenging to put others before ourselves. But it's also the most profoundly fulfilling, life-giving, breathtaking way to be alive. That's good news!

The Heart and Art of Loving the World with God

This book isn't so much about "doing mission." It's really about how we let God's will and purpose become our own. It's about making room for the character of God to be alive in us. What are God's character and purpose? Jesus announces it with these words from the prophet Isaiah: "The Spirit of the Lord is upon me, because he has anointed me to bring good news to the poor. He has sent me to proclaim release to the captives and recovery of sight to the blind, to let the oppressed go free, to proclaim the year of the Lord's favor" (Luke 4:18-19). Jesus then proceeds to do exactly what was written, and he chooses his first apprentices to learn and work alongside him.

Jesus calls and invites us to walk alongside him and learn his ways. Traditionally, the church has referred to this relationship-based practice as *discipleship*. Other disciplines and arts have referred to similar models as *apprenticeship*. Apprentices learn from a master teacher, and they learn not by sitting in a classroom for an hour or so each week but by walking and working with the master, asking questions, practicing what they've learned, being corrected, and practicing again and again. Apprentices do not simply acquire the technical aspects of a skill, but rather, they discover the art and heart of their discipline. Jesus, the master teacher, has shown and continues to show us how to be apprentices and how to teach others. Jesus teaches us the heart and art of loving the world with God.

Individuals and faith communities reflect the compassionate and loving God who sends us to love and serve. Albert Outler, one of the great theologians of the twentieth century, describes "the lives of men [and women] who have been led by it into joyous and unservile servanthood" who make the Word all at once tangible, visible, audible, and even winsome.[2]

God leads us as individuals and as communities to reflect the engaging grace and love of God revealed through Jesus the Christ and empowered by the Holy Spirit. We as Christians affirm this regularly and sacramentally. In our baptisms, we are commissioned, literally *co-missioned* with Christ, to a life in God's grace expressed through commitment to God's ministries in the world.

How many times during the sacrament of Holy Communion have we heard a pastor pray, "Pour out your Holy Spirit on us gathered here, and on these gifts of bread and wine. Make them be for us the body and blood of

Christ, *that we may be for the world the body of Christ, redeemed by his blood*" (emphasis added)?[3] God has poured out God's Spirit on us so that we can be the body of Christ in the world! These words mean we are entrusted with the ministry of Christ. Jesus' disciples are regular people, like you and me, whose lives are defined and shaped by God's love. We've experienced the grace of Jesus Christ and the power of the Holy Spirit. Our purpose is to be the continuing expression of God's love in the world. Our purpose—your mission and mine—is to love the world with God.

Additionally, the mission of the church—*our* churches and *every* church—is to love the world with God. We're not called to be an inert, status-quo institution but to be the living, breathing, serving, loving body of Jesus Christ!

So, are we ready to love the world with God?

Reflect

"Then their eyes were opened, and they recognized him. . . . Then they told what had happened on the road" (Luke 24:31, 35).

Ponder

Think of a time when your eyes were opened and you saw God in a new way. How did you feel? How did you respond?

Pray

As you take time to pray, ask God to open your eyes and your heart and to reveal the next steps on your journey.

Practice

How can you share with others your experience of God's love?
Where specifically have you encountered Jesus? Who was with you? How did it feel? What will you always remember from that moment?
What are three ways you might express Jesus' love to others?

2

Seeking the Kingdom to Come

The place God calls you to is the place where your deep gladness and the world's deep hunger meet.

Frederick Buechner

L ife is full of intersections. We encounter them all the time as we walk or ride a bike or drive from one place to another. An intersection is simply a place where two lines or paths or roads share the same space, where they cross each other. As children we were taught that when we cross a street at an intersection, we should look both ways because we may need to wait for or yield to oncoming traffic. Drivers know that intersections are both necessary and potentially dangerous. Drivers approaching an intersection must assess the situation: Should they slow down or speed up? What direction should they turn? These decisions are both in their own best interest (How do I get where I need to go?) and also in the best interest of others (How do I get there without causing harm to anyone?).

In our faith journeys, we come to intersection after intersection. We often find ourselves at crossroads that connect our lives with the lives of others. Sometimes these are moments of simple decision. Perhaps as we walk into the grocery store in December, we cross paths with a bell-ringing Salvation Army volunteer. In this situation, we quickly decide whether we will drop money into the metal basket. Sometimes we face more complex intersections, and we become unsure about how to respond. Almost daily, my commute takes me past men and women who stand on the street and hold signs asking for money. At such intersections, the persistent questions about poverty and homelessness collide with questions about justice and mercy. Nightly news reports remind me of suffering and loss in my own community and around the globe. Again and again, we find ourselves aware of "the world's deep hunger." How are we to respond?

On Earth as It Is in Heaven

In what we call the Lord's Prayer, Jesus teaches his disciples to pray by revealing the beauty, power, goodness, grace, and love of God. But this is only one side of the coin. The other side tells of our collective human longing, thirst, ache, and struggle. The Lord's Prayer reminds us that we live at the intersection of earth and heaven. The prayer invites us to the intersection of hurt and hope because that's where Jesus always seems to be. We have hurts and hopes, and we share the hurts and hopes of humanity. Jesus asks God to open our hearts to the realities of the world with the hope of transformation by saying: "Pray then in this way: Our Father in heaven, hallowed be your name. Your kingdom come. Your will be done, on earth as it is in heaven" (Matt. 6:9-10).

Several summers ago, I had the opportunity to visit Nigeria on a mission with members of the church I was serving. It was one of those extraordinary "You had to be there" experiences. When I returned home and tried to describe what I saw and felt and learned, I became painfully aware of the limitation of my words. Even photos and videos seemed inadequate to explain such an experience.

For one thing, Nigeria's landscape is gorgeous, which I was surprised and delighted to discover. The people, the moments of worship, the hills and fields, the jungle, the energy, and the music—all were stunning and breathtaking. More significantly, though, even in its beauty Nigeria can be distressing. During my trip, I also encountered vast poverty, orphaned children, and widespread illness. French philosopher and Christian mystic Simone Weil wrote, "There are two things that pierce the human heart. One is beauty. The other is affliction."

The intersection of beauty and affliction serves as a good place to begin the next steps of your journey with Jesus because that's where he spent much of his time. On lakeshores and mountainsides, at weddings, funerals, and dinner tables, Jesus shared the complexity of life with all kinds of people. He shared the pain of human experience and the hope for divine wholeness. He longed for wholeness and holiness to become our reality—"Your kingdom come. Your will be done on earth as it is in heaven." In other words, may the beauty of heaven—the goodness and rightness of God's will and God's way—become reality on earth among all people who live and love and hurt and hope. May God's righteousness, God's rightness, and God's justice and grace become as real on earth as they are in heaven. We pray for an active conformity to the will of God when we say, "Your will be done, on earth as it is in heaven." Every time we pray these words, we're asking God to make us participants in the building and cocreation of God's kingdom on earth.

Perhaps you've noticed that the Lord's Prayer is full of plural pronouns. Jesus reminds us that we're in this together, that God is *our* God—not just *mine*, not just *yours*. God claims us and knows that we have basic needs and hopes. We make mistakes and need forgiveness; we hold grudges and have a frightening capacity for hatred. We all need to practice forgiveness. For these reasons, we celebrate when others celebrate, and we hurt when others hurt. That's why our hearts are pierced by both beauty and affliction. No one escapes struggle or suffering. And all of us have the potential to experience the goodness, beauty, and joy of life.

We are all God's children, not just those of us who worship together. Jesus teaches us to seek God's goodness together—with and for and on behalf of one another. He teaches us to pray while looking through a lens focused on heaven and on God's design for humanity and all creation. Jesus asks us to look at the world through that holy lens, to look at ourselves and at others, seeing both views in one frame, one picture, one reality. If we imagine God's design for our lives and our world and we superimpose that over the world we live in, then we can watch God transform what *is* into what *shall be*. How do we pray for this kind of supernatural transformation? How do we pray, "Your will be done"?

How can we know God's will? When we pray the Lord's Prayer, we pray for God's kingdom to come and God's will to be done, and then we ask for our daily bread. The Old and New Testaments are full of images of feasts and banquets as a way of imagining God's kingdom. So maybe asking for our daily bread is more than a plea for our own daily needs. If the fundamental petition of the prayer is "Your kingdom come, Your will be done," and if the central appeal is for the coming of God's kingdom on earth, then perhaps this line means something like, "Give us this day a taste of the holy banquet," or "Give us this day a taste of God's kingdom on earth."

Well, we live in a hungry world.

As a child, I was often in the kitchen with my mother while she baked cookies or cakes. I couldn't wait to poke a spoon into the mixing bowl to get a taste of the uncooked mixture. That little taste was a kind of promise, an anticipation of the real thing. I believe Jesus wants his followers to have the same kind of appetite—an impatient hunger—to see God's reign on earth. The Lord's Prayer is an urgent request for a "taste" of God's kingdom—a taste of mercy, justice, and God's design and desire in the here and now. More than a prayer for daily food, the Lord's Prayer asks for something bigger, bolder, and holier.

When we recite the Lord's Prayer, we pray for God's reign to come and for God's will to be done on earth. We petition for just a glimpse of the day when all God's children will be fed enough that they can grow into healthy adults, a day when senior citizens will not have to choose among food or medications or heat in the winter.

Your kingdom come. God, give us this day a taste of your kingdom, your reign on earth—a hungry child being fed, a homeless family finding shelter—which will help us remember that when your will is done on earth as it is in heaven, hunger and homelessness will be no more.

Your kingdom come. God, give us this day a taste of your kingdom, your reign on earth—an abused or abandoned or enslaved child brought to a safe place—which will help us remember that when your will is done on earth as it is in heaven, child abuse and verbal abuse and domestic violence and human trafficking will no longer exist.

When this is our prayer every day, our eyes and our hearts will open to the goodness, mercy, and justice all around us. These small tastes will keep us going until the proverbial cookies are out of the oven.

When we petition God, saying, "Give *us* this day *our* daily bread," we are praying in a world where there is enough food to feed everyone but where 854 million people are malnourished and sixteen thousand children die from hunger-related causes every day.[1] We are praying in a nation where as many as thirteen million children under the age of twelve find it difficult to get enough food for physical and mental development. The kingdom that we ask God to bring is one of generosity and sufficiency that trusts God's daily goodness—a kingdom that replaces hunger with hope, a kingdom that meets real needs with real bread.

My friend and teacher Dr. Elaine Heath, an inspiring apprentice of Jesus, has learned and continues to learn the art and heart of loving the world with God, and she's an expert at teaching others how to do that too. She invites us to view the world through the hermeneutic, or lens, of love saying, "A hermeneutic of love is fully aware of the devastation of sin and evil, yet refuses to give them the last word."[2] In other words, we read the Bible and we also see the world, and when we look at both through the lens of God's love, we begin to see the deep need for grace, redemption, and hope.

Because we follow Jesus, we find ourselves again and again at that intersection where love and devastation come together, but we know that sin and evil will never have the last word. God has the last word. God, in fact, not only has the last word but also the first word and the living Word. What if we offered the living and life-giving Word made flesh in Jesus Christ to others? And what if we offered this life-restoring Word in tangible acts of companionship, shared food, clean water, and countless other small and large expressions of grace, hope, and love?

Our Unique Intersections

Now we stand at new intersections. We are in new places thanks to eye-opening, heart-opening experiences where our uniqueness and God's great purpose meet. In other words, God can use our unique lives in sacred ways that not only employ our gifts, abilities, and interests but also use them in ways that will bring joy to us and make a difference to others. But how can we know God's will and purpose for us? How do we do God's will? Discernment sometimes occurs in unexpected ways.

After his Chrysalis weekend, Daniel discovered new ways to use his God-given talents, interests, and questions. Daniel was a fifteen-year-old sophomore struggling with a decision about changing schools, trying to find the right fit. He described that Chrysalis weekend in the basement youth center of University Park United Methodist Church as "one of the most defining events of my life." He said that even more important than finding clarity about which school to choose, he found extraordinary joy. He marveled, "I'd never had that experience before."

Prayer became a real conversation with God, and in the prayer-filled days that followed, Daniel said, "It was refreshing to know where God was leading me. But actually doing it was hard." He became involved in a small group that functioned much like a Chrysalis or Emmaus reunion group in the way it provided weekly accountability and encouragement. Daniel was eager to express the sense of love and encouragement that he himself had experienced, and he soon volunteered to serve as a leader for subsequent Chrysalis weekends. He shared his own experience during the weekends and talked about what it means to be a Christian in the world using this beloved Emmaus story as an illustration:

> In Mainz, Germany, a beautiful statue of Christ stood with outstretched hands. During the heavy bombing of World War II, the hands of the statue were broken off. Following the war, a sculptor was hired to repair the statue, but the church members decided not to replace the hands. Instead they put a small plaque at the base of the statue reading, "Christ has no hands but yours."

The image of the handless Christ stayed with Daniel as he continued meeting with his accountability group, studying scripture, and praying. After his sophomore year in college, Daniel spent his summer working with underserved children in Dallas through Project Transformation. He experienced being the hands of Christ as he read and played with the kids at Casa Linda United Methodist Church. He loved the kids, and they loved him in return. He hoped to transform their lives, but he knows that they transformed his.

When Jesus says, "You shall love the Lord your God with all your heart, and with all your soul, and with all your strength, and with all your mind; and your neighbor as yourself" (Luke 10:27), he calls us to trade in our routines and our business-as-usual religion for a genuine, loving relationship with God. He calls us to a way of relating with others both inside and outside of the church with the same care and respect that we desire for ourselves. Being a disciple, following Jesus, and living a Fourth Day life, mean intentionally striving to make life better for others.

The *Walk* and the *Work*

During my trip to Nigeria, it took a couple of days for my ears to adjust to the unique accent of the Nigerian people. My team partnered with people who spoke English, but their accents had a strong British influence coupled with beautiful, almost musical, intonation. After a few days, their accents became easy to understand with the amusing and occasionally awkward exception of a few words.

One day we were visiting some church leaders in a remote village, and they kept talking about the challenges of the *walk* and the joys of the *walk*. Later we saw some people traveling by foot, and our leader told us how people often *work* great distances. It finally dawned on me that I was hearing two different words that sounded just alike: *walk* and *work*. But as we listened and learned and watched and worshiped, it became apparent that even though we were hearing two different words, one word was enough: To *walk* with God and to *work* with God are really the same thing.

As we walk and work alongside God, as we listen for God to speak into our hearts and lives, as we respond to God's presence and grace, we will be changed. We will find ourselves at a new crossroads; we will begin to think and see and act differently. We'll think and see and act in ways that reflect more of God's heart and less of our own. And we do these things in the belief that God's kingdom will come, on earth as it is in heaven.

Reflect

"Your will be done, on earth as it is in heaven" (Matt. 6:10).

Ponder

When you read the Bible or watch the news, what intersections do you notice that connect you with others? Where do you see both beauty and affliction in the world?

Pray

Each day for a week, pray the Lord's Prayer and focus on the phrase "Your will be done, on earth as it is in heaven." Pray that God will open your eyes to how the world should be. Where do you see physical hunger? Where do you see hunger for education or employment? Where do you see hunger for justice?

Practice

Think of five ways you might share Christ's love with others this week. Specifically, think about what you might do

to serve someone at home.

to serve someone at work or school.

to serve a local agency, charity, or nonprofit.

to serve a stranger.

to serve others in "fun" places; for example, a book club, the fitness center, a dance class, and so on.

3

First Things First

*But strive first for the kingdom of God and his righteousness,
and all these things will be given to you as well.*

Matthew 6:33

The first topic during an Emmaus weekend addresses priorities. Emmaus communities define the word *priority* as "a value, goal, relationship, cause, etc. of leading importance in your life. A priority is what you live for, what gives focus to your life. A priority is the shaping value around which the rest of your life tends to revolve. A priority is whatever has first claim on your time, energy, and resources. A priority is something you consistently prefer to (or feel you must) do, have, work toward, think about, or spend money on, above other possibilities."[1] Or as Bob Dylan simply puts it: "You're gonna have to serve somebody."[2]

Living as Christians is not about what we say we believe, where we show up to worship, or even what accomplishments we can boast. Either we live the unique lives that God asks us to live, or we don't. Either we give ourselves to and for others, or we don't. Either we choose mercy, justice, and love, or we don't.

The big questions aren't *What should I do?* or *How do I make time to serve?* or *What mission works fit into my life?* The questions are *How shall I live?* and *What kind of person will I be?* and *How do I love the*

Lord with all my heart and soul and strength and love my neighbor as myself? The prophet Micah wrote, "He has told you, O mortal, what is good; and what does the LORD require of you but to do justice, and to love kindness, and to walk humbly with your God?" (Mic. 6:8).

What do Micah's words mean for us?

What Matters Most?

In my conversations with people about their Emmaus experiences, a common theme emerges. I often hear, "When our speaker talked about priorities, it was like God was speaking directly to me!"

The PRIORITY Talk concludes with these questions: *What do you think about? How do you spend your money? How do you spend your time?* The answers to these questions reveal our priorities—who or what we worship. It's that simple. Let's put our books down for a few minutes and open our calendars. Let's take a look at our financial records. Study these records objectively. If we're feeling brave, let's ask someone to look at these records with us to tell us what they reveal. Time, money, and relationships are our greatest assets, and through them we make our most important investments.

Continue by asking the following questions: *Where does your time go? Where does your money go? In whom or what are you investing yourself? Whom or what do you serve?* This may prove to be a sobering or affirming exercise. It will most likely be some of both as we see what is important to us and also face those things that may be nothing more than distractions or diversions. Let us take some time to ponder and pray about the ways we use both time and money. May we practice compassion with ourselves. None of us has gone on to perfection just yet.

Our Stories and Our Witness

Ready for another challenging and eye-opening exercise? Let's try writing our own obituaries by imagining how we would summarize our lives. How would those brief paragraphs describe what matters most to us?

Many years ago I officiated the funeral of man named Malcolm whom I'd not met. I visited his family in an attempt to personalize his service. The first thing I learned was that Malcolm had alienated himself from most of his family. Tragically, he had put so much time and energy into his work and had placed so much emphasis on making and saving money that his wife and children used words like *miserly* and *mean* when they spoke about him. The more they told me, the more I pictured a Scrooge-like man. Later, I spoke with one of Malcolm's coworkers, a very kind gentleman who was obviously committed to the "If you can't say anything nice, don't say anything at all" philosophy. When I asked him to describe Malcolm, he thought for a moment and said, "Well, I'll tell you, Malcolm was pretty good at his job."

When the only positive thing that can be said about a human being created in the image of God is that he or she was "pretty good" at a career, I feel that something was missing in that person's life. I'm confident that God embraced Malcolm, and I said as much at his funeral in a nearly empty chapel. But I felt profound sadness that his life seemed mostly unlived, even though he died at an old age.

Andy, on the other hand, left his mark of joy on hundreds of people in his brief thirteen years. Andy simply loved people—he loved talking with people, helping people, playing and laughing with people. He made me a better person. He would show up after school in my office at church just to say hi or to tell me a joke. Sometimes he'd ask if he could help with anything. Sometimes he'd hug me with those sweaty, sticky, smelly, teenaged-boy arms of his. Sometimes he'd bump into my bookcases and knock things around. On Sundays he sang with the youth choir, and he'd often become giggly and distracted. Sometimes he'd fall asleep. Andy displayed an enormous capacity for kindness and justice. Simply put, he loved God and he loved people. Over two thousand people gathered to celebrate Andy's life because he had shared goodness with all of us.

What matters most isn't how long we live or how accomplished our lives might seem. What matters most isn't how much money or power we acquire. What matters most is how much of God's mercy, goodness, kindness, justice, joy, and love we share with others.

How do we want our lives to matter? What do we hope our families and friends have to say about us when we are gone from this earth? What do we want our obituaries to tell the world about how we spent our time? What kind of impact do we hope to have on the world?

Reflect

"You shall love the Lord your God with all your heart, and with all your soul, and with all your strength, and with all your mind; and your neighbor as yourself" (Luke 10:27).

Ponder

What matters most to you today? What do you *want* to matter most?

What one change could you make in your life in order to take a step closer to the life God calls you to?

How do people offer love to you in ways you never expected? How do you receive love that you didn't even know you needed?

In her poem "The Summer Day," Mary Oliver asks, "What is it you plan to do / with your one wild and precious life?" [3] How do you respond to that?

Pray

Prayer has been described as the language of lovers listening and speaking honestly and openly with the God who loves them most. To what or whom do you think God wants you to give your best attention and energy today?

Practice

Think of someone whose life has inspired you. If it's possible, ask that person to tell you about how he or she prioritizes life's demands and opportunities. What can you learn from this person's life?

Identify one action that you can take to reorder or protect the integrity of your priorities. Maybe that means beginning the day in quiet prayer, seeking a daily opportunity to bring joy to someone else, or giving your heart, time, and energy to others in a new way.

Keep a daily journal of how you spend your biggest assets: time and money.

4

Cultivating a Fourth Day Life

As you therefore have received Christ Jesus the Lord,
continue to live your lives in him, rooted and built up in
him and established in the faith, just as you were taught,
abounding in thanksgiving.

Colossians 2:6-7

As we live into our Fourth Days, we respond to our encounters with God out of our Emmaus experiences. We respond to the seeds God is planting in our lives. These seeds compel us to love and serve others in the name of Jesus Christ.

Terri is a wife, mother, attorney, tennis champion, and, above all, a Christ-follower. She describes her Emmaus experience and the transformation that followed this way: "I hate touchy-feely experiences. But my husband Ben had been [on a walk to Emmaus], and he encouraged me to attend. The aha moment for me happened in the discovery that so many people gave time, showered me with gifts, and provided committed leadership simply to show me love. Just to express love. Period. It was overwhelming."

Terri's Emmaus weekend planted the first seed of loving the world with God in her life. After that weekend, Terri knew she not only needed but also wanted to follow Jesus in serving and loving others. The seed was planted, yes, but Terri mentioned that she found it difficult to choose the next steps on her journey. Even so, she intuitively did what she needed to do. She carefully and intentionally listened for God. She listened for God by praying, studying scripture, asking questions, building relationships, and paying attention to the needs in her world. She cultivated her inner life—her prayer life and her relationship with God—and the fruit began to grow in her outer life. Our outer lives reflect our inner lives, which reflect our outer lives, and so on. Cultivating those tender seeds that God has planted within us will produce what the Bible calls the fruit of the Spirit: love, joy, peace, patience, kindness, generosity, faithfulness, gentleness, and self-control. God uses these qualities to produce tangible acts of service.

Cultivating our Fourth Day lives—serving others with God's love and compassion—is not unlike cultivating a garden. The ground must be prepared; the seeds must be planted. Sunlight, water, and nutrients provide the elemental gifts of life. Pesky weeds will grow and require removal. Eventually, the miracle of life emerges from tiny seeds. From dirt and dust, goodness appears. God has already prepared the fertile places in our lives. God has reached into the soil of our hearts to ready it to grow the fruit of a new season. God has spoken life into our hearts in bold and exciting ways.

Scripture often refers to seeds, weeds, vines, branches, gardens, and gardeners. In the beginning, God created life, and God continues to create and nurture life in and through us. Our hearts and minds have been moved, opened, and changed in many ways. We may even feel like a plow has worked its way through our hearts, turning the soil to prepare it for new growth. After living through a deeply spiritual experience, many say that they feel mixed up or vulnerable. In these exposed moments, may we remember that God often appears in the midst of change and chaos to breathe new life and plant new seeds. New life—that's what God promises and what we have received.

Cultivating Seeds

God has started a good work in our lives by planting some potent seeds, but that is only the beginning. As Paul writes to the believers in Philippi, "I am confident of this, that the one who began a good work among you will bring it to completion by the day of Jesus Christ" (Phil. 1:6).

How will we cultivate the seeds that God has planted in our lives? Many spiritual practices and disciplines can nurture these seeds, but here we'll explore the practices of prayer, gratitude, and generosity.

Prayer Cultivates Our Capacity for Reflection

As my friend Terri discovered after her Walk to Emmaus, prayer is a good place to start when seeking to discover and understand God's will. Some find prayer easy and natural; others feel like they are trying to speak a foreign language. And still others may find prayer irrelevant or futile. Perhaps we have found ourselves in all of those camps at various times in our lives. There have been days when I could only whisper "Please" in my own frustration and doubt. Other times I am able to exclaim deep praise and thanksgiving. And there have been more than a few days when the entirety of my prayer was, "Really?!" Yet, the most profound and transformational moments of prayer have come when I have quieted myself and listened for God.

God has planted small, tender, life-filled seeds in us, and now it is our job to listen carefully, to colabor with God in the cultivation of those good seeds. Prayer opens our hearts and minds for reflection and for listening to God in the deep places of our lives.

As a pastor, I'm often asked, "How should I pray? What's the right way?" The good news is that there are infinite "right" ways to pray. Throughout the Bible and history, conversations with God happened in all kinds of ways. Moses noticed a burning bush, and Elijah listened to deafening silence. Miriam sang, and David wrote poetic prayers that we still read in the Book of Psalms. Jesus frequently went to a quiet place, and he instructed his disciples to pray even for those who persecuted them. Paul implored followers simply to pray without ceasing. There are so many ways to pray that I don't believe we should worry about doing it "right."

Above all else, prayer is an open, honest, intimate conversation with the God who loves us most. Sometimes we speak; sometimes we listen. Sometimes we sit silently together; sometimes we petition God alone. No matter how or how often or where or when we pray, may we simply be open to what God reveals to us and then think deeply about any revelations that appear. Maybe God wants us to experience more grace so that we have more to offer others. Maybe God wants us to experience and extend more forgiveness. Maybe God wants us to have more courage or wisdom. We can trust that God will offer us what we need. Here are a few ideas for the types of prayer that invite reflection.

Breath Prayers

A simple and natural way to invite and welcome God's presence in our lives throughout the day is by praying short phrases or scripture. As we say or think a simple phrase, inhale and exhale deeply and slowly. This will help us quiet our minds and center our spirits. We might base a breath prayer on Psalm 46:10: "Be still, and know that I am God!" As we slowly inhale, pray "Be still," and then as we deeply exhale, pray "and know that I am God."

Slow and intentional breathing allows our minds and bodies to connect to our own spirits and to God's Spirit. Many people find this to be a simple yet powerful way of praying without ceasing, even through the demands and distractions of our busiest days.

Eyes-Open Prayers

As we go through the routines of our days, we encounter people and circumstances that remind us of God's presence and goodness. We also encounter people and circumstances that remind us that we live in a broken and struggling world. These experiences provide opportunities for instant, spontaneous prayer. On my way to work one day, traffic was slow because of an accident. Police and medical support were already on the scene, diverting vehicles to another route. I didn't know the people involved, but I could imagine their fear and pain. With my eyes open, I simply prayed silently, *Lord, thank you for being present to those who are injured and scared. Thank you for working through those who have responded. May each one experience a sense of your presence, comfort, and peace in these difficult moments.* When we come to God in an attitude of prayer and petition, the chaos that surrounds us is quieted—even if just for a moment.

Complete-the-Sentence Prayers

When I first began working as a youth minister, a colleague introduced me to "complete the sentence" prayers as a way of encouraging young people to articulate the prayers of their hearts, especially when they were shy or hesitant to pray aloud. My colleague invited the youth to complete a sentence—"God, today I'm thankful for . . . ." or "Lord, right now I'm really concerned about . . . ." As we read scripture or as we watch or read the daily news, pray, "Lord, help me understand . . . . " or "God, open my heart to . . . . "

However we pray, we'll likely experience God's presence within us more deeply, and we'll find that we are attentive to God's world in ways that help us carefully and thoughtfully reflect on how we can love the world with God.

Gratitude Cultivates Our Capacity for Delight

My colleague Rachel and I share mutual friends in the beautiful highlands of Guatemala. Not long ago, we looked at photos from her recent visit, and she shared this observation about the joy that comes from gratitude:

> From the moment our mission team set foot in the village of San Juan, we were greeted with joy-filled hospitality. After settling into our rooms, we walked to the compound. I was welcomed with a huge hug from my new and instant *amiga* Perla. Perla is a precious girl filled with love and joy, and her attitude instantly refreshed and renewed me. Perla's grandmother, Petrona, was our wonderful hostess and cook. She made amazing food and went to great lengths to make us feel at home. I encountered peace in Petrona and her family. Even though conveniences like water and electricity are sometimes erratic in her crowded home, Petrona finds deep joy. Regardless of her circumstances, she expresses

gratitude for what she does have and for God's presence, goodness, and love.

Rachel and I aren't the only ones who have basked in Petrona's joy-filled hospitality. Many who have visited San Juan have appreciated her radiant smile and her wonderful meals. And many have commented on her approach to life. Petrona experiences all of life as a gift, and she is grateful. Her gratitude is obvious; it shows in all that she does and says. Her smile is bright, her hugs are warm, and her prayers are heartfelt. She is grateful for each new day and for each person she encounters. She's grateful for the ways she experiences God's provision and mercy. Her life proclaims gratitude, and her gratitude is contagious. Just being in her presence makes me want to shout "Thank you!" to God.

Who or what makes you want to shout "Thank you!"? Who or what makes you want to say, "Look what God has done!"? Who or what makes you bow in silent gratitude because words are inadequate to express the gladness and thanksgiving that you feel? Who or what makes you want to call a friend, spouse, or loved one and say, "Guess what I just saw/felt/experienced that made me smile and laugh?"

Many people find writing about what they are thankful for in a journal is a great way to practice gratitude. Others vocalize their gratitude in a small group or with a spouse or friend. I know a young mom who expresses her own gratitude and teaches her children to do the same by naming something for which she is thankful every evening before dinner. I know a retired military officer who places his hand over his heart every morning and expresses his gratitude for his own life and for the lives of others. I know a young college graduate who compiled a gratitude list that includes the sound of rain, the smile of a stranger, access to running water, watching a puppy play, and the tenderness of his grandparents holding hands.

Gratitude expands our capacity for delight. Delight, joy, and happiness are gifts God wants to give us in all circumstances and in spite of our circumstances. When we express gratitude—when we find delight in God's goodness—we are freer to love and serve others. We are able to serve others not out of obligation or guilt but, like Petrona, simply because life is a gift meant to be shared.

Generosity Unleashes Abundance

In a little village called El Pescador ("the fisherman") in the Baja Peninsula of Mexico, a group of American students and adults finished their home-building work one evening, went back to their campsite, and warmed a huge pot of soup. They had worked hard all day mixing cement for the foundation of a small house, and they were hungry. As the sounds of laughter and the smell of the soup drifted into the village, a woman who lived in the community shyly approached the group. She and her four children were hungry. Her husband worked many miles away in a *maquiladora*, a manufacturing plant, and would not be home with his week's wages for several days. The work team invited the family to dinner. Word quickly spread throughout the town. Over the next hour, seven families joined the growing dinner group. The cooking team added additional water to the soup, praying it would stretch far enough to feed the big hungry crowd. One family brought fresh tortillas, and another brought two watermelons fresh from the garden.

We all know how the story ends. The new friends shared soup and tortillas until they could eat no more. Laughter and stories told in broken Spanish and English filled the air. Pointing, smiling, and sign language served as a wonderfully effective means of communication. Finally, the cooking team began to clean up and discovered they had more soup left over than capacity to store it. And so the soup went home with the seven families. How could there be so much left over? It didn't make sense. But that's what happened on a hillside above the Pacific Ocean in El Pescador, just like it happened two thousand years on a hillside above the shore of Galilee. Generosity unleashes abundance.

How can we practice generosity in a shaky economy and a culture of scarcity and fear? Simply by giving. By giving what we can and when we can, we trust that God still multiplies loaves and fishes.

For the more pragmatic among us, it might help to know that generosity is good for our health, and it makes us feel better. In a *Wall Street Journal* article published on August 31, 2013, author Elizabeth Svoboda reported on the work of neuroscientist Jordan Grafman who makes the case that we are hard-wired for giving. In other words, we are created to be generous. That makes sense to those who believe that we are indeed created in the image of a generous God. Dr. Grafman's research shows that the pleasure receptors of the human brain respond when people act generously. Acting generously feels good and right. And when we act generously, we discover that God's world is a world of more than enough—*abundance*.

The practices of prayer, gratitude, and generosity open us to seeing and loving the people and the world that God so loves. These practices nurture the seeds of a compassionate and a missional way of life.

Fourth Day Life Is Missional Life

Missional Fourth Day living participates with God in loving the world. It is seeing people as God sees people and loving people as God loves people. This way of life allows us to see and love people as if we were seeing and loving Jesus.

If we're honest, we may find it scary—risky even—to show God's love to others in tangible, personal ways. It's one thing to care about hungry and thirsty people. It's another thing altogether to figure out how to provide something for them to eat or drink. It's one thing to have compassion for the stranger, the lonely, the sick, or the incarcerated. It's another thing altogether to welcome, clothe, comfort, and visit them. We don't always know what to do or how to help. And even if we do know, we must be bold enough to take the risk of loving and serving others, knowing that we may not always see the impact we make. Loving the world with God *is* risky in all kinds of ways. And because it's risky, the practices of prayer, gratitude, and generosity are essential to staying grounded, centered in the love and purpose of God.

Fourth Day life is missional and fruitful. It strives to make a difference. Goodness and grace grow from Fourth Day living, and lives are transformed—beginning with our own. May we cultivate our Fourth Day lives, nurture them, and watch how God grows compassion in us!

Reflect

"A sower went out to sow. And as he sowed, some seeds fell on the path, and the birds came and ate them up. Other seeds fell on rocky ground, where they did not have much soil, and they sprang up quickly, since they had no depth of soil. But when the sun rose, they were scorched; and since they had no root, they withered away. Other seeds fell among thorns, and the thorns grew up and choked them. Other seeds fell on good soil and brought forth grain, some a hundredfold, some sixty, some thirty" (Matt. 13:3-8).

Take a few moments to read this excerpted passage along with Matthew 13:1-31. What does the parable of the sower say to you about your own life?

Ponder

Think about how and when you pray. How might you honor and cultivate your practice of prayer and reflection?

What did you say to the people you encountered today who supplied services to you? How did you practice gratitude?

Who is the most generous person you know? What can you learn from him or her?

Pray

For what are you grateful today? Tell God thank you! Ask God to reveal areas in your life where you can be more generous. Pray that God will grant you a joyful heart as you generously offer time, energy, and resources to others.

Practice

Think of two or three people for whom you are deeply grateful. Now write or call them. Tell them what you appreciate about them and why. Tell them how they've made a difference in your life.

Tell a grocery clerk, salesperson, or mail carrier how much you appreciate his or her efforts. What did you discover in the person's response? What did you learn about yourself?

5

Learning Practices for Mission

Jesus' hands were kind hands, doing good to all, healing pain and sickness, blessing children small, washing tired feet, and saving those who fall; Jesus' hands were kind hands, doing good to all.

Take my hands, Lord Jesus, let them work for you; make them strong and gentle, kind in all I do. Let me watch you, Jesus, till I'm gentle too, till my hands are kind hands, quick to work for you.

Margaret Cropper

Scripture is full of extraordinary stories of Jesus changing the lives of ordinary people through acts of compassion. Read the story of the paralyzed man and his bold friends in Mark 2:1-12. This story provides a powerful picture of the faithfulness of a few compassionate people acting courageously on behalf of a friend in need. Armed with God-given creativity and a spirit of courageous collaboration, the four friends showed their friend the love of God. We don't even know the names of the people in this story, but we can learn about Fourth Day life from them.

The Gospel writer's omission of the names of the paralyzed man and his four friends keeps our focus on Jesus as the protagonist of the story. Jesus is the incarnation of God's presence, the expression of God's love, the voice of God's forgiveness, the touch of God's healing power, and the invitation to God's abundant life. Jesus alone—not the disciples or the crowd or the unnamed paralyzed man or his friends—is at the center of this story. Jesus stands at the center of our own stories too as we seek to follow him. Given by God's love and empowered by the Holy Spirit, he is the model, teacher, pioneer, and perfecter of our faith. Jesus' loving presence and redeeming power invite and motivate the persons in the story and us to love the world with God.

Practicing Compassion

In Mark's account of the healing of the paralyzed man, we see people acting out of compassion. Perhaps that's because they've seen Jesus' compassion. Perhaps they too have experienced a word of forgiveness, a touch of grace, or a moment of healing in Jesus' presence. Now their friend is struggling—he's paralyzed. He can't do the things he wants and needs to do; he may feel helpless, hopeless, and depressed. These friends see Jesus and what he had done just a few days before when he healed a man with leprosy. The four friends reflect the compassion they see in Jesus as they literally dismantle a roof to bring their friend to him. They trust in Jesus' compassion and capacity to heal, and they commit themselves to getting their paralyzed friend within his reach. They reflect Christlike compassion. In their book *Compassion: A Reflection on the Christian Life*, Henri J. M. Nouwen, Donald P. McNeill, and Douglas A. Morrison write that when the compassion of Christ is within us, we will—like Christ—choose to be with people who hurt and share in their journeys.[1]

Practicing Creativity

We solve problems every day at work and at home. Some are no-brainers: If we're out of milk, we go to the store. If our cell phone is dead, we charge it. If our houses are messy, we clean them. But some problems require more thought—or even more hands and feet. The paralyzed man's friends find themselves in a challenging situation. But these friends are creative people. Because they can't enter the house in the conventional way, they think of a new plan—they remove the roof! We are creative by virtue of being made in the image of God, the Creator. Humanity has a long history of using this gift of creativity for great accomplishments. In this story we see faithful friends reflecting the creative nature of God and choosing to do a new and wonderful thing in the life of their friend. As many people today often face overwhelming and challenging obstacles, it's increasingly critical for compassionate Christians to find creative ways to meet their needs.

Practicing Collaboration

The compassionate and creative friends of the paralyzed man in Mark's Gospel exhibit the power of working together. These determined friends recognize that compassion alone isn't going to get this paralyzed man in front of Jesus. Even the best idea is inadequate if it can't be implemented. So they all work together. Imagine their conversation: "Maybe that roof plan is a good idea. You take him up there." "I can't carry him up by myself." "If we do it together, we can get him up there." "Then what? How are we going to get him *through* the roof?" "That could be really dangerous!" "Hey, I've got a rope. Would that help?" They all bring what they have—their ideas, their resources, their strengths. As they work together, they bring their friend to Jesus' feet.

Reverend Linda Roby, a mission-motivated colleague of mine, often reminds me that we work better together. She's right; we *are* better together. In 1 Corinthians 12, Paul describes the people who follow Jesus as a body. We are all part of one body—some are the ears and some are the eyes and some are the hands and some are the feet; yet we are interdependent. In the community of faith, we all need one another. Better still, when we help someone else experience God's presence, we often end up in a place where we experience it too.

Practicing Courage

Fourth Day Christians who work together to love the world with God need compassion, creativity, collaboration, and, finally, courage. Scripture talks a lot about courage. Over and over God says: Be strong and courageous.

Do not fear. I am with you. Throughout the book of Joshua, in the words of Isaiah, in the declarations of angels, in Jesus' teachings, and throughout the New Testament, we see and hear these words: Do not be afraid.

The friends of the paralyzed man acted with courage. They took risks, and they challenged the expectations of the community, all on behalf of one in need. The author of First John wrote, "Perfect love casts out fear" (4:18). Courage is the manifestation of love acting in the face of resistance, threat, or risk. The narrative in Mark's Gospel reveals the fruit of action motivated by love rather than fear. Perhaps these friends felt bold because of the courage they witnessed in Jesus.

Challenges and Demands of Fourth Day Life

The story of the paralyzed man and his courageous friends also shows us that Fourth Day life—loving the world with God—is both challenging and demanding because mission is messy. Life in that house in Capernaum was orderly and tidy, but now there's a hole in the roof. Jesus is teaching and preaching, the people are there to learn, and then the roof opens— definitely not part of the day's agenda. Mission can be both disruptive and inconvenient. Scripture is rich with stories about God interrupting plans and conversations and travels and jobs. Missional behavior is about God's agenda, not our own. God seldom waits for us to free our schedules in order to open our eyes and hearts. By definition, mission focuses on others. Therefore, following Jesus into the world means we pay attention to others.

Following Jesus is provocative. Many of Jesus' actions, such as those in Mark's Gospel, lead to questions, misunderstandings, skepticism, and doubt from his followers, the Pharisees, and anyone who hears of his miraculous works. When we get drawn into what God is doing, we should expect more questions than answers and more mystery than certainty. As we follow Jesus, we enter into a holy paradox. The church is the body of Christ in the world that reflects the love, grace, and power of Christ, but the church also searches for Jesus in the faces of the impoverished, the stranger, the hungry, the imprisoned, and the sick.

Loving the world with God is disorienting. As people encounter God's love—grace, forgiveness, healing, and new beginnings through Jesus—they begin to see themselves, others, and God from new perspectives. And in doing so, previously held assumptions are called into question.

How do we learn together to be both creative and collaborative as we seek to love the world with God? How do we seek courage so that we grow as people motivated and empowered by love rather than by fear?

Trading Judgment for Justice

At one time I assumed an unemployed person was lazy or, at best, inept at job-seeking. I once assumed an overweight person made poor eating decisions and rarely exercised. I used to assume that a person who cared for his or her home/car/clothes/children inadequately—using my own definition of what seemed adequate, of course—had some kind of character flaw. I once believed that a person in jail surely was guilty of something for which imprisonment is the appropriate consequence.

When we read the Gospels, we see Jesus encountering all kinds of people who struggle with the complexities and tragedies of life. He responds to their hurts and their hopes with deep connection, with kindness, and with a grace that restores and affirms dignity and humanity. In Luke 10, Jesus tells the story of the good Samaritan in response to a lawyer's questions. The lawyer undoubtedly has worked hard to avoid making mistakes. Maybe the lawyer, like me, has always assumed that if a person works hard enough and carefully follows the rules, he or she will experience success in life and even inherit eternal life. So Jesus tells this man a story that questions his assumptions and provokes a new way of seeing other people.

Jesus invites us to suspend judgment and simply see the needs of others. Unlike the religious leaders in the story—a priest and a Levite—the Samaritan sees the injured man as a fellow human being who is suffering and in need. The priest sees the injured man as a problem, maybe even as an impediment to holiness (if the injured man were indeed dead, the priest would be considered unclean if he touched the corpse). The Levite sees him as an interruption, a hassle. Both men are important, busy, and perhaps concerned that they will be unable to keep other commitments if they stop. To be honest, I can imagine and understand their rationale. It's logical, practical, and culturally congruent.

But Jesus invites us to practice countercultural ways of responding to those in need. Jesus constantly pushes against and through cultural norms to care for people just as they are. Jesus and the Samaritan in this parable don't do what many of us often do. They don't interrogate the suffering—How did you get yourself into this? Why did you take that road? Didn't you know it was dangerous? Why were you alone? Our culture blames victims or at least questions the motives and judgment of those who struggle. We blame the poor for their poverty and the hungry for their hunger. Nowhere in the Gospels do we see Jesus blaming a blind person for being blind or mourning family members for their grief. Jesus simply accepts people with compassion and responds in love and kindness. Surely we too can suspend judgment and extend grace to those who suffer around us.

If we're going to follow Jesus, then we'd do well to embrace God's gifts of compassion, creativity, collaboration, and courage. In doing so, we learn how to see people through Jesus' eyes—eyes that look for justice rather than for ways to judge.

Reflect

"As [Jesus] went ashore, he saw a great crowd; and he had compassion for them, because they were like sheep without a shepherd" (Mark 6:34).

Ponder

Whom have you observed practicing or embodying compassion? How do you receive and offer mercy?

In what ways might you collaborate creatively with persons for the sake of others?

When have you judged a person at first glance only to discover later that your assumptions were completely wrong?

When was the last time you were judged incorrectly? How did that make you feel?

What is the difference between judging and discerning?

Pray

Lord, make me an instrument of your peace.
Where there is hatred, let me sow love;
Where there is injury, pardon;

Where there is discord, harmony;
Where there is error, truth;
Where there is doubt, faith;
Where there is despair, hope;
Where there is darkness, light;
And where there is sadness, joy.
O Divine Master, Grant that I may not so much seek
To be consoled as to console;
To be understood as to understand;
To be loved as to love.
For it is in giving that we receive;
It is in pardoning that we are pardoned;
And it is in dying that we are born to eternal life.
Amen.

Practice

Write down words of judgment you use during the day and replace them with words of acceptance. For example, I sometimes think others are lazy, thoughtless, or self-absorbed. Perhaps I could also consider that they are deliberate, distracted, or focused. This helps me to remember that I cannot possibly know or understand all the challenges that another person may face.

Part II

Loving the World with God

*And Jesus said to them, "Follow me and I will
make you fish for people."*

Mark 1:17

6

Finding Our Starting Places

Religion that is pure and undefiled before God, the Father, is this: to care for orphans and widows in their distress, and to keep oneself unstained by the world.

James 1:27

I experience a recurring dream or vision on a weekly basis, more often in some cases. The dream takes place in a room at the church where I serve. There are people seated in the chairs around the room, and most know one another quite well. Because of that, their conversations are filled with insider language that unintentionally excludes any newcomers. The clock on the wall ticks slowly; time appears to crawl. An odd atmosphere of urgency mixed with boredom prevails. Two or three people in the room do most of the talking. Unfortunately, this isn't just a dream—it's a committee meeting. But that's not the worst of it.

In my head and heart, I hear a voice behind me. I turn and see Jesus standing in the doorway. He's been watching and listening, and he steps into the room to look each of us in the face. In a voice full of tenderness and agony—both fully divine and fully human—he speaks. "*What* are you doing? Who do you think you are, and *what* are you doing? This is *not* what I meant when I said 'Follow me.' This is not what I had in mind when I said I was hungry or cold or sick. This is *not* what I meant when I washed your feet and said 'Do this.'" An uncomfortable pause follows. No one speaks. Finally Jesus smiles tenderly and says, "Come love the world with me."

Jesus says, "Follow me" at least twenty-three times in the Gospel narratives. Over and over, Jesus invites the people around him to come with him, to join him, to be part of what he's doing. Over and over, he offers clear direction for living in God's grace and extending God's grace in ways that give life and hope to others. The writer of Hebrews calls Jesus "the pioneer and perfecter of our faith" (Heb. 12:2) and urges us to keep our eyes fixed on him.

The terms *disciple* and *discipleship* are familiar to us, and we know that a *disciple* is one who follows and learns from another, usually a leader. *Discipline* and *disciple* share the same Latin root *discipulus*, meaning "a learner." Let's think about the components of following and learning. How do we follow and learn? How do we invite others to join us? Where do we end up when we become a disciple, or follower, of Jesus?

I know where we'll end up when we become a disciple of Jesus: in our own neighborhoods, our communities, our churches, and completely new spaces filled with people different from ourselves. We'll make friends of all ages, colors, experiences, and perspectives. We'll see familiar people and places with new eyes. We'll encounter brokenness, pain, and injustice. We'll see hunger, addiction, fear, and loneliness. But we won't encounter these things alone. When we follow Jesus, we're with the one who offers hope, touches wounds, comforts grief, speaks compassion, uses courage, and bestows mercy. We may find ourselves in places of great affliction, but we won't find ourselves without hope. When we follow Jesus, we'll get a glimpse of the kingdom to come, a complex and colorful kingdom where all God's people are welcomed and loved.

Following Jesus is courageous, risky, adventurous, and thoroughly disruptive. Following Jesus is an act of trust-filled surrender to the discipline of love that ultimately frees us for a life of abundant mercy. Jesus warned and promised his first apprentices, "If any want to become my followers, let them deny themselves and take up their cross daily and follow me. For those who want to save their life will lose it, and those who lose their life for my sake will save it" (Luke 9:23-24).

Following Jesus is demanding, no question. Following Jesus into the world and loving the world with God will stress and stretch us. But it will also bring us unexpected and inexplicable joy.

Discovering Joy

Kim's Emmaus weekend came at a busy time in her life—so busy, in fact, that she considered not going. "My kids were small, my life was full, and, to be honest, it just seemed like one more thing to try to fit in." At the urging of others, she decided to go. "It wasn't really a mountaintop experience for me. I'm more reserved than some, and it was a little much." Smiling, she describes the unfolding joy that she discovered in the months that followed, as she surrendered more fully to following Jesus by loving others. "I found an incredibly deep and peaceful gladness. As I surrender and serve, I think I'm becoming more of who God calls me to be. It's what my life is supposed to be about."

A few years ago, for reasons I don't remember, I felt inspired to run a half-marathon. I bought a couple of books about marathons and read stories about great runners. I subscribed to *Runner's World*, and I read all about training for marathons. I signed up for classes at the local fitness center, and I listened to lectures about exercise physiology, nutrition, hydration, and how to buy the right shoes. I learned a lot about running marathons. I could have a very articulate conversation about aerobic capacity with actual runners. I was wise in the ways of distance running. But was I a marathoner? No. No, I wasn't a doer; I was merely a hearer of the word.

To become a marathoner, I would need to become a doer. I made myself get up, lace my shoes, get out the door, and stretch and sweat and gasp. I had to practice all those things I'd been reading and learning. And I couldn't do them just once—it would take a long time, doing them over and over. After the first week, I was not a marathoner. After the first month, I was not a marathoner. But slowly, by practicing and running more and more, my strength, endurance, and capacity grew. Eventually I finished a half-marathon. I wasn't fast, and running wasn't easy. But everything I'd read and learned became part of my experience. When I finally began to practice what I'd learned, the discipline became real, formative, and even transformative.

Runners run. Writers write. Teachers teach. But what about disciples of Jesus? We follow Jesus. That's what we do. Consider the words from James 1:22-25:

> But be doers of the word, and not merely hearers who deceive themselves. For if any are hearers of the word and not doers, they are like those who look at themselves in a mirror; for they look at themselves and, on going away, immediately forget what they were like. But those who look into the perfect law, the law of liberty, and persevere, being not hearers who forget but doers who act—they will be blessed in their doing.

We love and worship God by caring for people who suffer. We live out our Fourth Day experience by following Jesus as he reaches out to those who are hurting again and again. Jesus chooses to listen, touch, feed, hold, teach, honor, forgive, heal, and offer life to those who are hurting. And he invites us to follow, to learn from him, and to do the same. Following Jesus means going where Jesus would go and imitating Jesus where we can.

Seeing Who Jesus Sees

To learn practical steps that we can take on a daily basis—to order our lives after Jesus' example—let's look at what Jesus does in the Gospel narratives. Jesus pays attention. He really sees people—their uniqueness, their pain, their struggles, their failures, and their possibilities. He sees their hearts. What if we could see people the way Jesus sees?

Jesus goes out of his way. He crosses borders, and he breaks rules. He challenges the status quo. He challenges assumptions. He challenges authority, convention, and tradition. He provokes people. He loves people enough to do all these difficult things that our culture tells us not to do.

Jesus asks questions: What do you want? What do you need? Where are you going? What are you looking for?

Jesus empathizes and sympathizes with people. He feels deeply. The Gospel writers repeatedly use the Greek word *splagchnizomai,* which we translate as "compassion," to describe his response to the needs of others. *Splagchnizomai* means "to be deeply moved," literally "to feel pity in the depth of the bowels." Jesus cares deeply. He cries with us.

Yet Jesus also eats, celebrates, and laughs with people. He attends the wedding of his friends, and when the wine runs out, he turns water into really good wine! He eats with sinners and outcasts like Zacchaeus and Matthew and spends time with people who are considered unclean—those with leprosy, blood diseases, and mental illness.

Wherever he goes, Jesus extends God's mercy, power, forgiveness, and healing, and the most ordinary things are transformed—like water into wine. He opens the eyes of people who are blind, literally and figuratively, and releases people from whatever holds them captive. He transforms the lives of all he encounters, and he continues to do so.

Who wouldn't want to follow *that* Jesus? How can we learn to see who Jesus sees and to love who Jesus loves? It's a natural human tendency to be ethnocentric, judging other groups relative to our own ethnic groups or cultures, especially when it comes to language, values, practices, behavior, customs, and religion. We naturally define what's "normal" or "right" based on our own cultural contexts. As we gain more exposure and interact with other people, we learn about varieties of values, perspectives, languages, behaviors, and customs. And, hopefully, we discover that we have much to learn as we interact with others. Rather than making assumptions, people who follow Jesus will do well to do what Jesus does: engage in conversation, pay attention, and learn about the other.

A beautiful story unfolds in the fourth chapter of the Gospel of John. Jesus and his disciples are walking from one region to another, and the text tells us that "he had to go through Samaria" (John 4:4). In this familiar story, Jesus encounters a Samaritan woman at a water well and converses with her. The story reveals an extraordinary meeting that bridges several cultural divides: a Jewish man and a Samaritan woman, a Samaritan woman and the people in her own community, and ultimately the people of the community and the Messiah. Both Jesus and the woman act with courage, compassion, and collaboration. Their open and honest conversation fosters an almost impossible relationship between a Samaritan community and its Savior.

One of the best ways to grow in our understanding of other peoples and cultures is to note our assumptions, questions, observations, feelings, and reactions. Through journaling or in conversations with members of our reunion groups or study groups, we acknowledge and challenge our assumptions and move toward understanding. As my son's soccer coach

used to say to the perpetually distracted nine year olds: "Just pay attention, people!" Let us pay attention wherever we are—as we drive to and
from work, school, or church, as we watch the news or read the paper.

If we pay attention, we'll learn to see people as they are, not as we
think they should be. If we pay attention, we'll see Jesus when we see a
child who is hungry or thirsty. Or when we see an elderly person who eats
alone or not at all. Or when we see entire communities who don't have
access to safe drinking water. Or when we learn that people in entire coun-
tries spend as much as seventy percent of their incomes just to purchase
a small amount of food. When we actually see those people, we also see
Jesus.

When we see a stranger—someone who struggles to belong because
of differences in culture or language, or someone whose struggles often
go unnoticed—we also see Jesus. Do we see the person who picks up our
garbage or watches our kids at the school crosswalk or makes our latte? Do
we see the person who brings our mail or mows our lawn? Do we actually
see the person who sleeps under the bridge or begs at the intersection? Do
we see the refugee working menial jobs just to make ends meet? Can we
begin to pay attention and see the people who we sometimes fail to see?

Reflect

"The Son of Man came not to be served but to serve, and to give his life a
ransom for many" (Mark 10:45).

Ponder

Jesus says, "Follow me" at least twenty-three times in the Gospel narratives. How can you follow Jesus today? What makes you hesitant to follow
Jesus? What makes you eager to follow Jesus? What makes you too busy
to follow Jesus?
What gifts did God give you uniquely? How do you use those gifts?

Pray

Jesus went out of his way for others. Pray for God to lead you out of your
way to see and serve others.

Practice

Choose a day to change your routine. Take a different route to work or to school. Choose a route that takes you through an unfamiliar neighborhood. Who or what do you see?

7

Stepping Out of Our Comfort Zones

[Jesus] said, "Come." So Peter got out of the boat, started walking on the water, and came toward Jesus.

Matthew 14:29

In 1991, a group of thirty-four youth and adults, including myself, ventured across the United States–Mexico border from El Paso, Texas, to Juarez, Mexico, to build a house. We'd never built a house—in Mexico or anywhere else. We camped in the courtyard of a small church next to a busy road. The nights were cold, and the days were windy. We brought our own drinking water, prepared our own food, and hoped no one would get sick or hurt. I had assured the youth that we would build not *one* but *two* houses in four days. After our first full day of hard work, a high school junior named Jenny wondered aloud what many others were thinking. The conversation went something like this:

Jenny: Bec, this is hard. What if we can't do this? Do you think we can really finish these houses?

Me: Yes, I really believe that, Jenny. I could be wrong, but my experience and my confidence in all of you tells me that both houses will be finished by Friday.

Jenny: But we've never done anything like this. We don't know how. We're just kids. Do you really believe *we* can finish these houses? What if we can't do it?

Me: What if we *can* do it? What if we *do*? Imagine these two families having a warm, dry, safe home. Can you picture what that will be like for them and how it will change their lives?

Jenny: We are *so* going to finish these houses!

Like Peter on the Sea of Galilee, Jenny and her peers stepped out of their boats in the Juarez desert; they were in unfamiliar and uncomfortable surroundings, committed to a task they'd never done before with challenges they'd never encountered. They were invited to imagine a new reality that began to grow in them the desire and strength to bring the vision into being.

The Possibilities of *What If?*

What if those courageous kids had given up, resigned, or succumbed to their fears of failure? What if they had determined that this one house for this one family wouldn't change the face of poverty in Juarez? What if they had never seen and smelled the poverty of the *colonia*, the emerging neighborhood on the outskirts of the city, and what if they had closed their eyes and hearts to the needs of another family? They know they can't change the whole world, but they also know that they did change *that* family's world, and in doing so, their interior worlds changed as well.

I believe that asking *What if?* is a worthwhile spiritual practice. It keeps our eyes and minds open to what God is doing in the world, and it keeps us grounded as well. If we will simply follow Jesus into the world with a willingness to love, God will do the transformative work in us and in others. It may not look the way we expect it to look, and it may not happen on our time frames. That's okay because it's not about us. It's about what God is doing in the world. What if all of Jesus' apprentices imagined a world made whole and holy by the love and grace of God?

When we as followers of Jesus struggle with the power of *What if?*, we're empowered to confront the status quo (the structures, systems, and dynamics that oppress) with what might be (practices of justice, mercy, humility, and love), perhaps becoming part of the answer to the prayer: Your kingdom come. Your will be done, *on earth* as it is in heaven.

Following Jesus will stretch us, there's no doubt about that. Following Jesus will challenge us. And when we're stretched and challenged, when our spiritual and emotional walls get moved around or are dismantled altogether, we find ourselves living the adventure of faith.

Following Jesus means stepping out of the boat like Peter, trusting the one who calls to us, "Come on! Follow me! The water's fine!"

When we keep our eyes on Jesus and step out of the boat, risking our safety, our sanity, and our security, God is sure to show us something beautiful and powerful and holy.

What if we're open to that?

The Risks of *What If?*

"No one warned me," Paul said, "that it would be hard. There should be a warning."

Paul's Emmaus weekend in 2003 overwhelmed him. "I'd never in my life felt so loved, so completely and unconditionally loved. It was amazing. I was just saturated with this unconditional love, and I found myself compelled to learn to love like that. Before the weekend was over, I made a commitment that I would never pass by someone in need."

As Paul drove to his downtown office the very next Monday, he encountered several homeless people on street corners. "I know everyone says it's just the wrong thing to do, but I gave those guys a few dollars. I had promised God that I wouldn't just pass anyone by. But I didn't really know what to do."

That afternoon Paul bought some canned vegetables and meat, bottled water, and packaged cookies. He prepared small meal bags to keep in his car. The next day, when he encountered a homeless man in a wheelchair, he stopped and handed the man a bag of food. The gentleman peered into the paper bag and then looked quizzically at Paul. "I don't have a can opener," the man said. "Do you?" Paul's moment of joy became a scavenger hunt as he tried to find a can opener somewhere in the downtown office complex.

An hour later, having finally bought a can opener in a convenience store, Paul drove back to the corner where he'd last seen the man in the wheelchair. As he pulled to the curb, he saw a policeman questioning the man. Stepping out of his car, Paul approached the two men and said, "What's going on?" The officer replied, "Oh, this guy tells me he's just waiting for someone to bring him a can opener! Can you believe that?"

Paul pulled the can opener from his pocket, smiled, and said, "That would be me." The police officer shrugged and laughed, got in his car, and drove away.

Paul still carries bags of food in his car, but he's careful to always provide cans with pull-tops. And he says it's still hard to follow Jesus. Today he's the Executive Director of a nonprofit ministry that serves and supports struggling pastors in Africa. Paul acknowledges there's never as much money as there is demand, never as many volunteers as there are needs. He often wonders what the future will hold, but he never doubts that God will provide for the ministry's needs, and he chooses to be part of that, even when it's hard.

The Gospel of Matthew reminds us that following Jesus might sometimes mean stepping out of our comfortable boat of the familiar into the fluid and uncertain reality of life. Jesus said to the men in the boat, "'Take heart, it is I; do not be afraid.'" Peter answered him, 'Lord, if it is you, command me to come to you on the water.' He said, 'Come.' So Peter got out of the boat, started walking on the water, and came toward Jesus" (Matt. 14:27-29).

Following Jesus is risky. We probably will have to step out of our comfort zones. And loving the world with God is iffy business. We will face frustrations, questions, and discouragement. What if we give our time and energy to others in need, but we don't see any results? What if we work hard for mercy and justice, and it doesn't seem to make a difference? What if we get up at four o'clock in the morning to provide breakfast at a shelter, and no one thanks us? What if we spend all day building a wheelchair ramp for an elderly couple, and they never smile at us? What if we go to Guatemala to build a clinic, but we come back with an infection? What if we follow Jesus into the world to share the mercy and love of God, and it just doesn't look like the kingdom has come?

To put it plainly, taking risks for God's kingdom will frustrate and discourage us. But taking risks in response to God's love and the needs of others will change the world. Following Jesus into the world will challenge us emotionally, physically, relationally, and spiritually. We're likely to feel overwhelmed or even disillusioned. We may feel inadequate or ill-equipped. And we're right. We *will* be inadequate and ill-equipped if we forget that God works alongside us.

Scripture provides powerful narratives to inspire, encourage, and lead us into new ways of engaging with others and with the world. Moses leads people from oppression; David faces a giant; Daniel faces lions; Paul faces persecution. But the overarching story of scripture is the story of God's faithful love redeeming creation. And Jesus invites us to be part of that story. As we enter into unfamiliar and uncomfortable places, may we remember the stories from scripture of other people just like us who faced seemingly insurmountable obstacles in their faith journeys.

Following Jesus is difficult. Mission is messy and unpredictable. Fourth Day living changes us from the inside out. Loving the world with God is risky.

Okay, fine. Let's do it anyway.

Reflect

"Peter answered him, 'Lord, if it is you, command me to come to you on the water.' He said, 'Come.' So Peter got out of the boat, started walking on the water, and came toward Jesus" (Matt. 14:28-29).

Ponder

Imagine taking an action that really frightens you. What is it? What are two or three things you would undertake if fear were not a factor?
When have you been invited "out of the boat" to try something new or risky?

Pray

Pray this week about God's dreams for the world. Pray "Your kingdom come. Your will be done, on earth as it is in heaven" when you see someone in need, when you watch the news, when you hear about a need in your community, or when you learn of a natural disaster in a faraway place. What if Jesus asked you to respond? What would that look like?

Practice

Find out what your faith community is doing to serve others either locally or globally. How can you contribute?

Call a local food pantry, shelter, clinic, or school and ask what their most immediate needs are for support, volunteers, or donations. Step out of the boat and do something. (Hint: It's okay to invite someone to step out of the boat with you.)

8

Bringing Grace to Relationships

Amazing grace! How sweet the sound.

John Newton

S andra described her surprise when she volunteered to read with students at a school in one of Dallas's poorest neighborhoods. "I went to read with a fourth-grade boy, and I hoped that maybe it would be helpful to him, that maybe he'd improve his grades, maybe he could be an exception to the rule in that school, in that part of town. I guess I thought I could change something for him. But after just a few weeks, I realized he was changing something for me. He changed me. He changed the way I see children. He changed the way I see poverty. He changed the way I see myself. He changed the way I see God."

In our Walk to Emmaus or Chrysalis weekends, we discussed and explored the many ways in which God extends grace. We pondered God's ever-present *prevenient grace* (the grace that comes before any human decision or endeavor), *justifying grace* (God's yes to us in creation and on the cross and our yes to the relationship God offers us in Jesus Christ), and *sanctifying grace* (the work of the Holy Spirit in and through us). These aren't different kinds of grace but different ways of expressing, describing, and understanding the way God's love works in our lives. John Newton's classic hymn calls God's grace amazing, and it is!

Many people describe another experience of grace when they serve others in the name of Christ. A young nurse said, "I went with my church's team to Guatemala thinking I would help build a clinic or teach a skill to someone there. I had no idea that I would receive so much more than I could possibly give!" An elderly companion shared, "All I did was sit with a friend in the hospital before her surgery. We didn't even talk very much. But she told me later that she felt God's presence. I know I did. I don't understand, but it was a holy moment."

Practicing Grace in Relationships

God's grace flows both ways, doesn't it? Just when we think we're extending it to someone, we discover that it's coming right back at us multiplied, amplified, and revealing more and more about ourselves, other people, and about what God is doing in the world. God reveals extraordinary grace and goodness in and through our relationships.

Over time I have learned that listening to God *with* and *through* others is essential, particularly when we attempt to serve others. We may not be our most loving and serving selves when we assume to know what is best for another person or another culture, and we may do harm rather than good when we impose our own beliefs based on those assumptions. The author of Hebrews wrote, "Do not neglect to show hospitality to strangers, for by doing that some have entertained angels without knowing it" (Heb. 13:2). How can we show hospitality as we love and serve others?

For example, if we were to collect and deliver food or supplies to the homeless that were not needed, wanted, or helpful (even if we believe they *should* be), we create frustration, confusion, distrust, and probably more work for the recipients. We may inadvertently create new challenges in our efforts to meet tangible needs. Mother Teresa of Calcutta said, "Today it is fashionable to talk about the poor. Unfortunately it is not fashionable to talk with them."[1]

Talking with—not about—others enables us to hear their needs and hopes and also learn what God is already doing and how we can participate. Jesus' example invites us to talk with the hungry, the outcast, the frightened, and the overwhelmed. Like Jesus, we will hear stories of hurt and of hope. Through friendship and conversation, we learn about the lives of others, and we begin to see through their eyes and understand their hearts. We learn to be neighbors, friends, and partners together in meeting needs and showing loving in tangible ways. Grace-filled relationships teach us to engage with others in ways that may make us feel exposed. When we approach any relationship with our questions, doubts, weaknesses, biases, fears, and insecurities as well as our best intentions, we enter into sacred spaces where God is at work.

Years ago, as the youth group from my church planned a trip to Mexico to build a little house, one of the most influential mentors in my life said, "You know, this isn't about a *trip*." Inundated as we were with van rental agreements, permission slips, health forms, luggage, tools, and the requisite supply of snacks for the journey, I looked at him with the smallest bit of skepticism. "It *looks* like a trip," I responded.

Mission does sometimes look like a trip—or a meal, a blanket, a service project. But mission is not fundamentally about trips or projects or meals or blankets. Trips and projects have a beginning and an end. Missional Fourth Day living is the experience of relationships that continue to form and transform lives long after the soup is served or the vans are unpacked. Trips and projects have budgets and objectives; missions have heart and connections and relationships. Mission is a way of being alive in the world, letting God live in and through us, creating community, finding purpose, and offering Christ's hope and grace to the world!

Listening Builds Relationships

Jesus initiates conversations and asks questions in order to build relationships. He asks, "What do you want me to do for you?" and "What do you see?" and "Who do you say I am?" Conversations and questions help us to look both within and beyond ourselves for understanding.

In the process of listening to God and to one another, we can foster authentic relationships that allow us to hear and express deep hopes, hurts, needs, and dreams. I appreciate the way Elisabeth Schüssler Fiorenza articulates this:

> Relationships are not built on the transfer of money and resources, but rather on an exchange of hopes, fears, and life stories. Christian spirituality means eating together, sharing together,

drinking together, talking with each other, receiving each other, experiencing God's presence through each other, and in doing so, proclaiming the gospel as God's alternative vision for everyone . . . especially those who are poor, outcast, and battered.[2]

Questions and conversations are essential practices for grace-filled relationships because we're all learners and teachers, followers and leaders, at different times and in different ways. I've learned that when a group is embarking on any missional experience, it's not only important for me to listen to the participants' questions but also equally important for me to ask questions that provoke curiosity or inquiry or even discomfort. That's how I learn.

For example, when my church group goes to a low-income neighborhood in South Dallas, I ask the members of the group how many grocery stores or libraries they notice. I ask why they see a different array of goods and services in various parts of the city and what that says about our community. Voicing our own questions gives others permission to do the same, and we have the opportunity to learn together, much like we did during our Emmaus experiences.

Together we can ask real questions in the context of grace-filled relationships. Together in a safe environment, we can challenge old assumptions, explore new ways of thinking and acting, and experiment with creative and collaborative approaches to faithful discipleship.

The central questions we ask in missional Fourth Day living are these: Who is my neighbor? How do we live as neighbors? How do I love my neighbor as myself?

The mission of the church expresses our life together as the body of Christ in which every person has a gift to offer. (See 1 Cor. 12:12-27.) All people, no matter their situations, have a deep need to give and to have their gifts received and validated.

Even in small ways, everyone can share his or her God-given gifts. Ann, who works in older adult care, invites Alzheimer's patients to arrange the flowers in the vases on the dining room tables of the assisted-living facility each day. Kay, who works at a West Dallas community center, asks the older adults there to help fill the snack bags for hungry kids. The three-year-olds in my church draw pictures and make cards for our pastors to take on hospital visits. The homebound members of my church take pride in praying for others in the church. Everyone has something to offer as well as the capacity to receive the gracious gifts offered by others. What if we approached every encounter with someone as an invitation to experience and share God's grace?

Reflect

"Send out your bread upon the waters, for after many days you will get it back" (Eccles. 11:1).

Ponder

Think of a time when you've experienced a grace-filled relationship. What was that like? What did you experience and learn?

Where and how do you experience the body of Christ at work in the world?

Pray

Pray about your own vulnerability. How open are you to confessing your own questions, needs, or brokenness to God and to others? How open are you to receiving grace from God and from others?

Practice

When you feel you need something during the day, try offering it to someone else. What emotions do you experience through the act of giving?

Make note of your responses when you experience goodness and grace from someone else.

Part III

Learning and Acting in Community

And let us consider how to provoke one another to love and good deeds, not neglecting to meet together, as is the habit of some, but encouraging one another, and all the more as you see the Day approaching.

Hebrews 10:24-25

Better Together

If you want to go fast, walk alone.
If you want to go far, walk together.

African proverb

Amy, Cyndie, and Karen have been meeting every Thursday morning for coffee and conversation for twenty-two years since their Emmaus experiences. Together they have navigated different life stages—marriage, motherhood, sickness—and even a three-year period when Cyndie lived in Yemen, and they hosted their meetings online. These weekly moments are an anchor, a source of strength and inspiration, and the friends have no intention of stopping because, as Amy adamantly says, "God knows we need one another!"

Amy is right. We *do* need one another. We're better together. Our shared life shapes us as Fourth Day people. Even the most independent or introverted among us needs the support, encouragement, accountability, prayer, grace, and presence of others on our journeys. We may belong to covenant groups, accountability groups, life groups, or group reunions. We might meet in homes, churches, coffee shops, or parks. We may meet with three people or with thirteen. But we all need people who share our journeys, our stories, and our hearts.

The author of Hebrews reminds us of the importance of encourage-ment and meeting together often to discuss how we love and serve others. (See Hebrews 10:24-25.) These aspects are key components of our Fourth Day journeys.

"It's a safe space, sacred really," Mitch tells me. Mitch is a successful businessman who manages projects with extraordinary grace and effec-tiveness. "I learned how important it is for people to be heard, to contrib-ute," he says of his Emmaus experience. "Everyone has a story. Everyone has an idea. Everyone brings something to the table." Mitch noted that he even uses some of the Emmaus weekend practices of discussion, playful-ness, and creativity with his coworkers "to build trust and community. We're just all better when we do that."

One of the key commitments and practices of Emmaus participants is the group reunion. This is a small group, usually just two to six members, consisting of those who have been pilgrims on an Emmaus or Chrysalis weekend. Ideally, a group reunion meets weekly. This is a covenant group, though it may be called by a variety of names: accountability group, dis-cipleship group, share group, etc. The group's purpose is to help people persevere and grow in faith, to learn together and encourage one another as they take the next steps in following Jesus.

The Power of Community

Part of the power of a small group (reunion, covenant, or accountability) is the ongoing work of encouraging one another to think deeply and to pro-cess actions and feelings. Each time we step out of our comfort zones and into the messy and sacred world of caring about others, we risk stepping in the confusion of humanity. We may find ourselves asking questions about God and about this world filled with both beauty and affliction. When we share our journeys and questions with one another, our capacities to love and serve with humility, faithfulness, gratitude, and grace grow.

Our Emmaus or Chrysalis weekends were seventy-two-hour expe-riences of deep Christian community and fellowship, what the New Testament calls *koinonia*. *Koinonia* is described in Acts 2:42: "They devoted themselves to the apostles' teaching and fellowship, to the break-ing of bread and the prayers." Throughout our weekends, we did just that. We spent time together exploring scripture, praying, and learning what it means to be loved and claimed by the grace of Jesus Christ. For many people, this is a new and profound experience.

We may experience a similar dynamic when serving with others in mission. Again and again, mission participants have remarked on the unexpected transformative power of small-group relationships that have been formed by mission experiences. Even in large groups of fifty or one hundred persons, meaningful connection can be fostered through the intentional use of small-group processes. Community is built and strengthened when we serve together.

The body of Christ is a community infused with God's power by the Holy Spirit and commissioned by Jesus to love the world with God. Experiencing a community working together on behalf of others can be life-giving and life-altering. On the other hand, if community life is not carefully nurtured, participating in a mission experience may result in little more than a nice service project. Following Jesus into the world entails a journey that may take us to unfamiliar people and places and lead us to a deeper understanding of ourselves. This journey is too challenging and too important to walk alone.

The Gospel narrative of the paralyzed man and his friends provides a powerful image of a compassionate and courageous community seeking wholeness for another. As we observed earlier, by keeping God's love through Jesus Christ at the center of its story, the community of faith will be empowered by the Holy Spirit to behave collaboratively and creatively. As Christians, we have the privilege and responsibility of fostering, cultivating, and nurturing this particular kind of community. That's why group reunions, covenant groups, shared worship and service, and intentional spiritual friendships are essential to growing in discipleship.

Scripture and experience show us that compassion, creativity, collaboration, and courage are fostered in the context of community through the practices of hospitality, worship, and sacrament. Authors Hugh Halter and Matt Smay wrote, "The call of community isn't about finding people just like us. . . . Community in the biblical sense is clearly about unlike people finding Christ at the center of their inclusive life together."[1]

How can we cultivate our shared life so that we really are better together and better able to love the world with God? Through the community practices of hospitality, worship, and sacramenal living, we nurture and grow our missional lives together.

Hospitality

Hospitality is an umbrella term for a broad variety of service industries including but not limited to hotels, food service, casinos, and tourism. The hospitality industry is huge, and it's just that—an industry, a commodity. And because it is such a huge industry, we forget sometimes that hospitality originated in the ancient faith traditions. Hospitality, at its core, is about how people treat one another. Hospitality stems from the recognition that every person is God's creation and a gift. Hospitality, therefore, speaks to how we honor and care for one another.

Scripture reminds us that practicing hospitality reflects God's love and goodness and opens us to receiving grace and creating relationships. (See Romans 15:7 and Hebrews 13:2.) Carol tells this story of modern-day scriptural hospitality:

> Last fall, some women from my congregation joined women from all over the country to work together on several houses in southern Louisiana after a hurricane. One of the homeowners that we met was a young woman named Susanna. She and her husband had three little girls, and the house they lived in was about the size of a single car garage, just barely standing. On the third day, Susanna told our group that she'd like to provide lunch for us. There were sixteen people working on her house, and it was apparent that she didn't have the means or the space to feed us all. But at lunchtime, she invited us in. Her daughters stood at the doorway and welcomed us, and when we went into the house—six at a time—we squeezed around the table that just barely fit between the stove and the bed. She had prepared the table so carefully. She offered each person a cold Coke, warm bread, and delicious soup. She was not only friendly and gracious but also radical in her hospitality. She invited us in as strangers so that we could become friends.

Henri J. M. Nouwen defines *hospitality* as "the creation of a free space where the stranger can enter and become a friend instead of an enemy."[2] The world we live in is sometimes hostile, sometimes indifferent, often lonely and confusing. So many people feel isolated from friends, family, and God. As Christians, we have an incredible opportunity to offer open and welcoming emotional and physical space where strangers can become friends. When we open ourselves—specifically when we make space as God's people *for* God's people—we will find that God is our host!

When we share safe and friendly spaces, we create places and moments where everyone is free to search and to question and to seek God's presence and meaning. Hospitality does indeed create community and build unity on the shared confession of our mutual brokenness and on the affirmation of our shared hope. People who practice hospitality are door-openers, conversation-starters, smile-givers. Disciples who practice hospitality live in an openhearted way at home and at work, in the church and in the community.

Mark and Janice open their home each week to their neighbors to share soup, bread, and life. The get-together carries no expectations, except that they be present in one another's lives as neighbors. Another couple, Dennis and Dana, picks up three of their widowed friends to go eat burgers together on Friday evenings. They choose to share their lives with a few people who might be facing a lonely weekend. A local church practices hospitality by sharing its space with a nonprofit adult education group. Another shares its parking lot and bus with a small school across the street. Hospitality need not be complicated. But it does need to be genuine.

Worship

We're better together when we worship together. Worship gives us the chance to see and celebrate what God is doing—in, through, beyond, and sometimes in spite of us. Here's the key: When we worship God, we surrender ourselves and offer our praise and reverence and love to the Creator of the universe. We proclaim in song, prayer, silence, sacrament, and word that God is good and that we value God above all.

Jesus told the woman he met at a well, "But the hour is coming, and is now here, when the true worshipers will worship the Father in spirit and truth, for the Father seeks such as these to worship him. God is spirit, and those who worship him must worship in spirit and truth" (John 4:23-24). Worship engages our hearts and heads and hands to love and honor God.

When we come together to let prayer, scripture, song, and sacrament speak into our lives, we nurture God's gifts in one another and foster the strength of our faith to be Christ's hands and feet beyond the walls of our sanctuaries or chapels.

Ricky shares this story about his experience of connection and community when he participated in a weekend mission team:

> It was the weekend before Christmas, and I was working with a *Labors for Neighbors* team in Sabine Pass, Texas, to get a roof on a hurricane-battered church. It wasn't a convenient time for anyone on the team, and it was certainly uncomfortable for those who were on the roof, although no one said so. We were silently aware of the months of distress that this congregation had endured since mid-September—more than three months of cleanup and a roof still leaking.
>
> We arrived late morning on Saturday in a cold drizzle. We made introductions, heard our work and safety instructions, and prayed, and then things got busy on and around the roof. It seemed so big, maybe too much to complete in the next twenty-eight hours, especially when we considered that it would be dark and cold for nearly twelve of those hours. The roof *was* big but not as big as the community of people that God gathered together on, under, and around that roof. Church members and community residents came by with hammers, food, and smiles and joined us on the roof, in the kitchen, and in laughter. At dusk, someone mounted a bright floodlight on the roof, and the hammers continued their percussive rhythm. Our new friends shared their stories about Hurricane Rita—how they prepared, how they evacuated, what they returned to, and what they lost. Cynthia told us about living in a tent before moving into a small room in the church's education building. Ralph told us about the generosity of people who themselves had very little. Debbie, quietly and with wet eyes, offered cobbler.
>
> On Sunday we took a mid-morning break to join the congregation for worship in the small, weather-torn sanctuary. We sat on folding chairs set on a stripped floor, light pouring in through braced and still partly boarded windows. Doris, the organist, played Christmas hymns on the surviving electric piano, and we sang. We sang the sweet familiar words of promise, hope, birth, and incarnation.

"How silently, how silently, the wondrous gift is given," we sang, "so God imparts to human hearts the blessings of his heaven." Wondrous, indeed, this little church opening its big heart to us. Wondrous, surely, this community of hospitality and laughter. Wondrous, to get to be in a place where God's presence is evident and freely shared. Wondrous, yes, to realize that the roof would be completed. More wondrous still to recognize that, as important as the roof was, something more essential, more basic was happening in that moment. "O come to us, abide with us, our Lord Emmanuel!"

Sharing our lives with others while God chooses to be in the midst of it—that *is* a wondrous gift! How amazing to be a small part of God's big world and to see the love of God made flesh. How amazing to stand in a small church and sing about God's love arriving as a helpless infant. How amazing to climb onto a roof and look out over a small community that claims God's enormous presence. May we praise God for experiences such as this.

Sacramental Living

Fourth Day living invites a sacramental way of seeing life. Life is holy, created by God, and so each moment has a sense of sacrament, of sacred meaning. Sacramental life is sacrificial life. Both words—sacramental and sacrificial—share the same root *sacer,* meaning "holy." Life is sacred and holy—not just on Sunday mornings or in Bible study. As baptized Christians, we are initiated into the body of Christ and into the work of God in the world. We're commissioned and invited to share God's mission of loving the world into redemption. My friend Betty likes to say that we're commandeered—that God's call and claim on our lives are so compelling that we can't even resist. But I have to respectfully disagree; the gift of free will means that we *can* resist, and God knows we do! The real issue in being *commissioned* is our willingness to be *submissioned,* that is, to live under God's mission. A truly sacramental life is a sacrificial life submitted to God's will. It is in community that we are reminded that God's will and not our own ultimately claims our passion, energy, and hearts.

When we come together in our shared identity as people created, redeemed, and empowered by God, we find our deepest sense of self and our strongest sense of connection with others. When we share in the baptism of another, we reaffirm our own sacred place in God's world, and we declare the sacred role of others. And we do it together, remembering that God initiates and writes this story that we share.

A common congregational response to baptism gives us the opportunity to say, "With God's help we will so order our lives after the example of Christ, that this person, surrounded by steadfast love, may be established in the faith, and confirmed and strengthened in the way that leads to life eternal."[3]

How will we "so order" our lives each day?

Reflect

As your Emmaus weekend concluded, you were reminded: "Life in grace is not a destination. It is a journey for the sake of the world. Life in grace is not a satisfactory lifestyle to be achieved. It is a pilgrimage of love that never ends in this life. . . . Remember, you have an essential role to play."[4] You are called to be the leaven in the dough, the salt of the earth, the light in darkness. (See Matt. 13:33; 5:13-16.)

Ponder

At what moment this past week did you feel closest to Christ? At what moment during this week did you feel you were responding to God's call to be a disciple? How did you participate as a member of the body of Christ this week?

Pray

Ask God to open whatever it is in your life that is closed—your home, your heart, your church.

You may wish to use this prayer: Come, Holy Spirit, fill the hearts of your faithful and kindle in them the fire of your love. Amen.

Practice

List your activities for the day. Where can you include an element of hospitality, worship, or an awareness of the sacred?

What support do you need from your spiritual community? How can you offer encouragement to someone else?

10

Reflecting and Acting

Any fool can know. The point is to understand.

Attributed to Albert Einstein

One way that God works in us is through our own life journeys and in the many ways we learn, adapt, stretch, grow, adjust, ask questions, and engage in new ways with the world. Our relationships with God continually restore us, impart new life to us, perfect us in the image and likeness of God, and equip us to love the world with God. We were reminded of this in the SANCTIFYING GRACE Talk during our Emmaus or Chrysalis weekends.

> Sanctifying grace produces both the desire and the power to give God our undivided attention—our whole heart—and our entire life. . . . Our focus shifts from being self-directed to being led by the Spirit of God. With Christ, we take our place on the front lines of issues that affect all of God's children and the world God created for us. . . . Sanctifying grace is the journey toward wholeness and holiness made possible by the working of the Holy Spirit. This grace imparts to us the very mind, heart, and hands of Christ so that we can love our neighbor as ourselves.[1]

The image of the three-legged stool helps us envision a balanced Christian life. Piety, study, and action are the outward expressions of our internal lives of prayer and devotion, learning, and submission. These aspects of the inner spiritual life are closely connected and are reflected in the ways we live our lives each day.

As Christians learning to follow Jesus into the world, we find ourselves adapting to new experiences, new people, and new thoughts and feelings. Our experience changes us, and then we engage a little differently with the world.

Here's an example of how we might encounter this change: Concrete experience (serving a meal at a shelter and meeting a young mother) is followed by personal reflection on that experience (recognition of her humanity and struggle). This reflection is followed by an abstract understanding (internalizing the injustice of a young mother's dilemma of choosing between paying rent and buying food for her child), which is then tested through further experience (meeting with a volunteer at a social services agency to gain insight), which leads to the next concrete experience (returning to the shelter to learn more about the young mother). I call this an action-reflection-next action process.

Each new experience invites us to learn, to think about what we've learned, and to incorporate what we've learned into our lives. Remember those crucial questions at the conclusion of the Emmaus weekend: What has this meant to you? What are you going to do about it? These questions beg to be asked whenever we experience or encounter God's work in our lives and in the world.

Exploring these experiences, observations, and questions with your group reunion or small group will help you, as well as those in your group, to grow and cultivate Fourth Day lives. As we follow Christ into new places and experiences and listen to what the Spirit says, we learn, reflect, and stretch our understanding. We're compelled to keep following Jesus, growing deeper in love with God's world, growing deeper in understanding, growing deeper in trust, and moving deeper into places of both struggle and serving. God is always inviting us to richer life experiences.

A Presbyterian pastor named Steven serves as a mentor to me. Steven is a natural, graceful skier, and I learned to love the slopes of Los Alamos, New Mexico, by following him down steep trails. He didn't tell me what to do, and I didn't think about what I ought to do; I just followed him. Eventually I became a more competent skier. Maybe that's what Jesus asks of us: "Walk with me and work with me—watch how I do it. Learn the unforced rhythms of grace. . . . Keep company with me and you'll learn to live freely and lightly" (Matt. 11:29-30, THE MESSAGE). When we "keep company" with Jesus, through prayer, study, and action, the Holy Spirit continually works in and through us, equipping us to love and serve others with energy and joy. And when we do that with other disciples, we find encouragement, courage, strength, and joy for our journeys.

When we have the opportunity to serve, we might find that questions like these help us reflect more deeply on our experiences, allowing us to grow in awareness as we love the world with God:

What does this tell me about human nature?

What does this tell me about the world?

What does this show or teach me about grace?

What does this reveal about justice or injustice?

What scripture does this experience evoke?

What does this opportunity reveal about the body of Christ at work in the world?

How can I act justly in this situation? How can I show mercy?

How does my reading of scripture inform how I react to the needs of others or when I observe injustice?

Reflect

"'Do not judge, and you will not be judged; do not condemn, and you will not be condemned. Forgive, and you will be forgiven; give, and it will be given to you. A good measure, pressed down, shaken together, running over, will be put into your lap; for the measure you give will be the measure you get back.'

He also told them a parable: 'Can a blind person guide a blind person? Will not both fall into a pit? A disciple is not above the teacher, but everyone who is fully qualified will be like the teacher. Why do you see the speck in your neighbor's eye, but do not notice the log in your own eye? Or how can you say to your neighbor, "Friend, let me take out the speck in your eye," when you yourself do not see the log in your own eye? You hypocrite, first take the log out of your own eye, and then you will see clearly to take the speck our of your neighbor's eye'" (Luke 6:37-42).

What does this say to me about where to begin in understanding the ways God might use me to love the world?

Ponder

What do you need to examine in your own life? What "logs" can you identify in your own eyes?

In a group reunion or small group, make a list of additional questions to
ask one another specifically related to experiences of serving others. For
example: What has made submission to God's will hard for me this week?
What has encouraged me to be committed to God's justice in the world this
week? Where have I experienced joy this week?

Pray

Pray for God to work both in your head and in your heart to deepen your
understanding and to grow you in wisdom.

Practice

Journal each day. Be specific as you record your actions; your observations; your feelings; what you've discovered about yourself, about God, and
about the world.

Examine how your experiences and discoveries impact your actions and
your way of seeing and relating to others.

Examine how prayer, scripture, and worship impact your actions.

Explore the ways your experiences and discoveries impact the way you
experience prayer, worship, and scripture.

Share these discoveries and insights with another person.

11

Sharing Stories of God at Work

I love to tell the story, 'Twill be my theme in glory,
To tell the old, old story of Jesus and His love.

A. Katherine Hankey

I just held the light," Karyn told us, describing her work in a free clinic in an inner city. "The doctor was cleaning the man's wound, and the power went down in the clinic. It was dark. Someone found a flashlight, and so I held it while the doctor cared for the gentleman. I just held the light."

That's really what we're all called to do, isn't it? God does amazing things through amazing people, and sometimes we get to be there—to hold the light, to tell the story. We get to point toward God, and say, "Look! Look what God has done!"

Emily Dickinson's wisdom still rings true: "The Truth must dazzle gradually / Or every man be blind."[1] Let's tell the stories of God's goodness and power, and let's tell those stories in ways that dazzle without blinding!

Here are some suggestions for sharing what God has done:

Tease with questions: In worship, in church newsletters, or on a church website, post some "Did you know . . . ?" questions. *Did you know that when you spend forty-five minutes of your time reading with a child, you improve her chances for academic success? Did you know* *there are children in Guatemala who don't have access to immuniza-tions? Did you know that in sub-Saharan Africa, ten dollars provides a malaria-preventing bed net? Did you know that seven people from your church provided breakfast for 450 hungry students last week?*

Let pictures tell the stories. Select a few great photos—pictures that show relationships and connections or that reveal shared faith and hope—and create a "mission gallery" in a church hallway. Publish the photos in a church newsletter. Invite those in the photos to give a brief description of what they experienced.

Tell other people's stories. The most servant-hearted people are often unlikely to toot their own horns. But their stories are beautiful and deserve to be told. At a casual dinner not long ago, I listened in awe as my friend Sam told the others at the table about the faithful and persistent work of his next-door neighbor, who tirelessly directs an after-school pro-gram for children in an underserved area. The neighbor would never have mentioned the years of work or the pouring of his own resources into this ministry. He wouldn't have described himself as selfless or sacrificial or Christlike. But he is, and his story wanted to be told—not to glorify him-self but to point to what God can do through everyday disciples.

Let the stories tell themselves. To be honest, as we become more and more faithful about loving the world with God, we won't need to tell stories. At the end of the day, if we've nurtured relationships and honored, protected, loved, and given our best to make a difference, the stories will tell themselves. The rocks and stones will cry out. Neighborhoods will look different. Jail census will look different. Disease statistics will look differ-ent. People's lives will look different.

On a bright Saturday in March, as spring break finally arrived, a long caravan of seventeen vans lined up to cross the border from El Paso to Juarez. The vans were loaded—I mean *packed tight*—with 140 students from Texas A&M's Aggies in Mission group. Ready to spend their spring break building homes for the poorest of the poor in Ciudad Juarez, they had filled the passenger vans with peers and the cargo vans with the food, water, tools, and camping gear necessary to create a small community on the high desert.

As the caravans approached the Mexican customs gates, our repre-sentative from Amor Ministries, the agency with whom we worked and built in Juarez, told us that we needed to be attentive to which lane we used. Normally, he said, we would go through the *Nada por declaracion* (Nothing to declare) lane, but today, because of the size of the group, the customs officers had asked us to enter through the lane marked *Por declaricion*. So even though we were clearly a noncommercial group with nothing to declare, we lined up as requested and passed without incident into the streets of Juarez and on to the compound where we'd be living for the next few days.

The next Friday morning, these same students—a little tired, a little dusty, and more than a little transformed—packed up the vans for the return trip, eager to cross back into El Paso for their first hot shower since leaving College Station. Before we loaded up, the student leaders gathered everyone together for a time of prayer, song, and sacrament. Student after student shared their experiences: "I saw God in the gentle spirits of the family that we were building with." "God's power was so evident in the way this diverse group was able to work together." "Did you see how God opened the heart of that young father at the house we worked on?" "I can't quite put my finger on it, but I know things will be different because I'm different now."

Luke's Gospel tells a story about a young man being healed of a multitude of problems. At the end of that story, the young man begs to stay with Jesus, but Jesus sends him home: "Return to your home, and declare how much God has done for you" (Luke 8:39). After breaking the bread (tortillas) and sharing the cup (Welch's), after giving thanks for all that God has done, and saying yes to the invitation to get out of the boat again and again, this amazing group of young adults got back on the vans and headed home. Regardless of the customs lane our vans would pass through on the return journey, these young disciples had much to declare to the world!

Shouting or Silence?

In the Sermon on the Mount, Jesus says to let our good works shine like a bright light on a hilltop and in the very same sermon says that we shouldn't be showy about practicing our faith. (See Matthew 6:1-4.) What? How does *that* work?

Again, the wisdom of Micah speaks: "What does the Lord require of you but to do justice, and to love kindness, and to walk humbly with your God?" (Mic. 6:8).

When it comes to serving others, it seems people or groups tell their stories in two ways. Some never say a word. Others tell everyone all about what they've done, how much they've sacrificed, how many times they've gone to Nepal or Kenya or Honduras, how many people they've recruited or rescued, how many houses they've built, or how many souls they've saved. I'm guessing Jesus wouldn't endorse either of these communication plans. On one hand, he tells his disciples to do their good works secretly, and on the other hand, he tells them to let their lights shine.

Cory's Walk to Emmaus energized him in ways that surprised him. When his church's mission council announced a summer mission opportunity in Peru, he was one of the first to sign on. He continued to be surprised by what he heard and learned as the team began their preparations. He listened with curiosity as Lyn described a comment heard at the Lima airport a year earlier as their team waited to board a plane for their return flight home. "We were in the gate area waiting for our flight, and it was very crowded, of course. There were lots of conversations going on around us in several languages. But one caught my attention when I heard a Peruvian man say, 'Look at all the missionaries in their T-shirts. Who do they think they are? They come in and tell us what's wrong, and then in a few days they leave. I wish they would just stay home.'" Lyn went on to tell the group how important it was to hear those words. "What we say and do will stay in Peru long after we leave. What stories do we hope they'll tell after we come back home?"

Cory says that was a pivotal conversation. Their team worked hard to "begin with the end in mind," always asking, *What stories will they tell after we leave?* They prayed long before they ever arrived in Peru that the people with whom they worked would tell exciting stories—stories of God's goodness and mercy, stories of hope, and stories of transformation.

If we're faithful to God by following Jesus and loving others, then we'll give people reason to echo the psalmist: "I will extol you, my God and King, and bless your name forever and ever" (Ps. 145:1).

Living Our Fourth Day, Today and Every Day

As our three-day Emmaus experiences concluded, we as pilgrims heard a final talk called FOURTH DAY. The speaker wanted to remind us that just like those first disciples encountered Jesus on the road to Emmaus on that first Easter day, we too have encountered and experienced Christ in distinct and profound ways. And just like those first-century Christians, our relationships with God through Christ are not only for our own sakes but for the sake of a world that hungers and thirsts for love, justice, hope, and wholeness. The speaker reminded us that "the purpose of The Walk to Emmaus is to inspire and equip you to be a disciple whose heart burns with the love of God, who will bring new vision to your church, and who will return with renewed commitment to offer Christ to the world in which you live."[2]

Now every day is our Fourth Day. Every day offers opportunities to know and celebrate God's grace and to share it with others. Every day we find opportunities to encourage other Christians and to receive their encouragement for our daily walks. Every day we have opportunities to love and serve the world that God loves and to point to the ways that God redeems and transforms life. Every day is our Fourth Day—our day to love the world with God.

As we stay focused on our priorities—loving God and loving others—we will cultivate our capacities and abilities to carry out God's work in the world. As we spend time in prayer, seeking God's kingdom on earth as it is in heaven, and deliberately cultivate compassion for others and the courage to take action and serve, we'll discover both the strength and the joy to be exactly who we were created to be. We'll discover that Fourth Day living is challenging, and God will sometimes nudge us and stretch us in surprising ways. We'll see God at work in our communities or maybe far away, and we'll discover our own ways to be a part of God's plan.

God *so* loves the world—and we get to love the world *with* God!

Reflect

"You are the salt of the earth; but if salt has lost its taste, how can its saltiness be restored? It is no longer good for anything, but is thrown out and trampled under foot.

"You are the light of the world. A city built on a hill cannot be hid. No one after lighting a lamp puts it under the bushel basket, but on the lampstand, and it gives light to all in the house. In the same way, let your light shine before others, so that they may see your good works and give glory to your Father in heaven" (Matt. 5:13-16).

Read Psalm 107 and underline or circle the experiences with which you resonate most.

Ponder

Earlier in this chapter, we read "Return to your home, and declare how much God has done for you" (Luke 8:39). Would you rather hear someone describe what they've done or what God has done? Why?

Think of a time when you heard someone talk about what he or she has accomplished or sacrificed. How did that make you feel? How did that point or fail to point toward God?

What have you seen God do this week? How can you tell the story and keep the spotlight on God?

Pray

This ancient Hebrew prayer invites us to see God's work and to celebrate it:

Days pass and years vanish, we walk sightless among miracles.
God, fill our eyes with seeing and our minds with knowing.
Let there be moments when your presence, like lightning,
illumines the darkness in which we walk.
Help us to see wherever we gaze that the bush burns unconsumed.
And we, clay touched by God, will reach out in holiness
and exclaim in wonder, "How filled with awe is this place and
we did not know it!"

Practice

What's your story? How has God shown mercy and love to you?

What have you seen God do in your world today? Make note of moments of joy, connection, or hope. Share these moments with others.

Whose story can you tell today to point toward God's goodness?

How will your life be a living testament to God's love at work in the world?

NOTES

Introduction

1. From "The Great Thanksgiving," *The United Methodist Hymnal* (Nashville, TN: The United Methodist Publishing House, 1989), 10.

Chapter 1

1. "Talk #15: FOURTH DAY" *The Walk to Emmaus Talk Outlines* (Nashville, TN: Upper Room Books, 2004), 165.

2. Albert Outler, *Evangelism in the Wesleyan Spirit*, (Nashville, TN: Tidings, 1971), 101. Outler's book is the transcription of four lectures delivered in 1971 at the United Methodist Congress on Evangelism in New Orleans, Louisiana. This quote comes from the fourth and final lecture, titled "A Church of Martyrs and Servants."

3. From "The Great Thanksgiving," *The United Methodist Hymnal* (Nashville, TN: The United Methodist Publishing House, 1989), 10.

Chapter 2

Epigraph: Frederick Buechner, *Wishful Thinking: A Theological ABC* (New York: Harper and Row, 1973), 95.

1. http://www.umcor.org/Search-for-Projects/Projects/982920

2. Elaine Heath, *The Mystic Way of Evangelism: A Contemplative Vision for Christian Outreach* (Grand Rapids, MI: Baker Academic, 2008), 124.

Chapter 3

1. *The Walk to Emmaus Talk Outlines* (Nashville, TN: Upper Room Books, 2004), 12.

2. Bob Dylan, "Gonna Serve Sombody," *Slow Train Coming* (Special Rider Music, 1979).

3. Mary Oliver, "The Summer Day," *New and Selected Poems* (Boston: Beacon Press, 1992).

Chapter 4

1. Elizabeth Svoboda, "Hard-Wired to Give" *The Wall Street Journal*, August 31, 2013.

Chapter 5

Epigraph: Margaret Cropper, "Jesus' Hands Were Kind Hands" (Stainer & Bell, Ltd., 1979).

1. Henri J. M. Nouwen, et al. *Compassion: A Reflection on the Christian Life* (New York: Image, 1983), 27.

Chapter 8

Epigraph: John Newton, "Faith's Review and Expectation, Hymn 41" *Olney Hymns*, 1779.

1. Mother Teresa, *Mother Teresa: In My Own Words*, comp. José Luis González-Balado (Liguori, MO: Liguori Publications, 1997), 23.

2. Elisabeth Schüssler Fiorenza, *In Memory of Her: A Feminist Theological Reconstruction of Christian Origins* (New York: Crossroad, 1994), 97.

Chapter 9

1. Hugh Halter and Matt Smay, *The Tangible Kingdom: Creating Incarnational Community* (San Francisco: Jossey-Bass, Leadership Network Series, 2008), 149. The authors' reference to discipleship as apprenticeship has been a significant influence in my thoughts regarding missional formation.

2. Henri J. M. Nouwen, *Reaching Out: The Three Movements of the Spiritual Life* (New York: Image, 1986), 71.

3. Baptismal Covenant II-B, *The United Methodist Book of Worship* (Nashville, TN: The United Methodist Publishing House, 1992), 105.

4. "Talk #15: FOURTH DAY" *The Walk to Emmaus Talk Outlines* (Nashville, TN: Upper Room Books, 2004), 163-172.

Chapter 10

1. "Talk #12: SANCTIFYING GRACE" *The Walk to Emmaus Talk Outlines* (Nashville, TN: Upper Room Books, 2004), 132.

Chapter 11

Epigraph: A. Katherine Hankey, "I Love to Tell the Story" *The United Methodist Hymnal* (Nashville, TN: The United Methodist Publishing House, 1989), 156.

1. Emily Dickinson, "Tell all the truth but tell it slant" from *The Poems of Emily Dickinson: Reading Edition*, ed. Ralk W. Franklin (Cambridge, MA: Harvard UP, 1999).

2. "Talk #15: FOURTH DAY" *The Walk to Emmaus Talk Outlines* (Nashville, TN: Upper Room Books, 2004), 166.

CPSIA information can be obtained
at www.ICGtesting.com
Printed in the USA
LVHW03s0949260818
587849LV00008B/81/P